What's a Nice Girl Like You Doing in a Relationship Like This?

Women in Abusive Relationships

Edited by Kay Marie Porterfield

THE CROSSING PRESS
FREEDOM, CA 95019

Copyright © 1992 by Kay Marie Porterfield

Cover design by AnneMarie Arnold

Printed in the U.S.A.

Library of Congress Cataloging-in-Publication Data

What's a nice girl like you doing in a relationship like this?
   edited by Kay Marie Porterfield.
         p.   cm.
   ISBN 0-89594-493-6. -- ISBN 0-89594-492-8 (pbk.)
   1. Women--Literary collections. 2. Abused women--Literary
   collections. 3. Interpersonal relations--Literary collections.
   4. American   literature--Women authors. 5. American
   literature--20th century. I. Porterfield, Kay Marie.
   PS509.W6W45 1992
   810.8'09287' 09045--dc20   91-34740
                                                        CIP

ACKNOWLEDGMENTS

Thanks to all the women who have touched my life over the years, to Dylan McPherson for his morale-boosting sense of humor and to Jacob George for his eye for accuracy and detail.

Renee A. Ashley: "Bone" originally appeared in *Carolina Quarterly*, Winter 1985. Reprinted by permission of the author.

Carol Barrett: "Calculatin'" originally appeared in *The Prose Poem*. Reprinted by permission of the author.

Marilyn Elain Carmen: "First Marriage Again" originally appeared in *Impetus Female Only 3*. Reprinted by permission of the author.

Marie Cartier: "Chronicle of Violence" originally appeared in *Athena*, Winter/Spring 1990 and in the *1987 Alternatives to Family Violence Appointment Book*. Reprinted by permission of the author.

Naomi Feigelson Chase: "What's Good About The End" originally appeared in *Negative Capability*, Winter 1991. Reprinted by permission of the author.

Donna Decker: "Tree Rings" originally appeared in *Gender and Society* (Sage Publications, Inc.). Reprinted by permission of Sage Publications, Inc.

Denise Duhamel: "The Night Before Father's Day" originally appeared in *Downtown*, Spring 1990. Reprinted by permission of the author.

Nancy Izawa: "Man!" originally appeared in *Perceptions, Pronouncements and Judgements: Feminist Poetry*. Reprinted by permission of the author.

Linda Keller: "Bullies" originally appeared in *Up Against the Wall Mother*, April 1987. Reprinted by permission of the author.

Paula Legendre: "Rodin's Lovers" originally appeared in *Just Between Us* and *Cokefish*. "Two Month Anniversary" originally appeared in *Up Against the Wall Mother* and *Perceptions*. "Pedestal" originally appeared in *Just Between Us, Pegasus and Cokefish*. Reprinted by permission of the author.

Chris Mandell: "Thoughts After a Rape" originally appeared in *Call It Courage: Stories Battered Women Tell*. Reprinted by permission of the author.

Cris Mazza: "In Six Short Lessons" originally appeared in *New Letters*, 1989, and *Is It Sexual Harassment Yet* (Fiction Collective Two) 1991.

Anne Meisenzahl: "The Lone Woman" originally appeared in *Negative Capability*, December, 1991. Reprinted by permission of the author.

Caitlin Morrel: "Stripped Surrender" originally appeared in *None of the Above (NOTA)*, Spring 1990. Reprinted by permission of the author.

Elisavietta Ritchie: "Elegy for the Other Woman" was originally published in earlier versions in the *New York Quarterly, The Unicorn in the Garden, Uncle, Raking Up the Snow* and *Off My Face*. Reprinted by permission of the author.

CarolAnn Russell: "Kitchen Meditation" originally appeared in *Malahat Review*, Number 92, 1990. Reprinted by permission of the author.

Laurel Speer: "What We're Thinking When Rapture Doesn't Happen" originally appeared in *Ink 6*. Reprinted by permission of the author.

Sharon F. Suer: "Too High a Proof" originally appeared in *Impetus Female Only 3*. Reprinted by permission of the author.

Patti Tana: "A Name and a Face" originally appeared in *Matrix: Women's Newsmagazine*, January 1990. Reprinted by permission of the author.

Fabian Worsham: "Null and Void" originally appeared in *North of Wakulla: An Anhinga Anthology* (Anhinga Press), 1989. Reprinted by permission of the author.

Contents

Foreword / *Lenore Walker*   VII
Introduction / *Kay Marie Porterfield*   XI
Love Song / *Willa Koretz*   XV

Growing Pains

Carrots in Their Pockets / *Iris Litt*   2
The Night Before Father's Day / *Denise Duhamel*   3
A Letter Refusing the Inheritance / *Jo Jane Pitt*   5
Tree Rings / *Donna Decker*   12
Hooks / *Karen Bowden*   14
Jessie / *Elspeth Cameron Ritchie*   16
Why I Am Wanting to Solve Every Echo Because /
Beverly G. Merrick   21

Dark Enchantments

Null and Void / *Fabian Worsham*   24
The Astounding Capabilities of the Human Mind /
Candice Rowe   26
Disappeared / *Barbara Foster*   33
In Six Short Lessons / *Cris Mazza*   34
Stabbing / *Nancy J. Wallace*   43
A Mind of Winter / *Yona Zeldis McDonough*   45
First Marriage Again / *Marilyn Elain Carmen*   54

Love Betrayed

One Hit to the Body / *Mary Shen Barnidge*   58
Blackmail / *Susan Hawthorne*   59
The Crush / *Eileen Elliott*   60
Honeymoon / *Rusane Morrison*   67
Kitchen Meditation / *CarolAnn Russell*   69
Looking for a Home / *Ceil Malek*   71
Again / *Barbara Ittner*   75
Married Love / *Marilyn Zuckerman*   77
Going to the Store / *Ann Bronson*   78
Suspicion / *Phillis Gershator*   81
Spilled Milk / *Pamela Pratt*   82
What We're Thinking When Rapture Doesn't Happen /
Laurel Speer   84
Evening... / *Nina Silver*   86
Supervision / *Karen Leslie*   87

Ruined / *Suzanne Grieco* — 93
Thoughts After a Rape / *Chris Mandell* — 94
A Name and a Face / *Patti Tana* — 95
Leaves / *Nancy Lott Gauld* — 100
Stripped Surrender / *Caitlin Morrell* — 101
Sentiment for All Seasons / *Joanne Seltzer* — 102
The Stain / *Vickie C. Posey* — 104
Bone / *Renee A. Ashley* — 108
how it feels with half the loaf / *s.l. wisenberg* — 109
The Concert Master / *Barbara M. Simon* — 111
MAN! / *Nancy Izawa* — 113
Vines / *Mary Crescenzo Simons* — 114

Breaking the Spell

The Past / *Lynn Leone* — 116
Chronicle of Violence / *Marie Cartier* — 117
Now Look What You Have Done / *Cheryl Townsend* — 119
Flashbacks / *Elayne Clift* — 120
Elegy for the Other Woman / *Elisavietta Ritchie* — 128
Chains / *Ellen E. Behrens* — 129
Too High a Proof / *Sharon F. Suer* — 133
Walking Wounded / *Norma Blair* — 134
Bullies / *Linda Keller* — 138
Calculatin / *Carol Barrett* — 140
A Friend's Confession / *Gina Bergamino* — 142
Releasing / *Judith Serin* — 143
2% / *G. Marault* — 148
Notes from the Ex / *Meredith Moore* — 150

Healing

Finally Breaking Training / *Alison Stone* — 160
A Circle of Voices / *Elizabeth Weber* — 161
Words...Just Words? / *Rochelle Natt* — 163
The Lone Woman / *Anne Meisenzahl* — 168
Letting Go / *Tama J. Kieves* — 169
Death and Life / *Paula Legendre* — 177
Daily Lessons / *Ahn Behrens* — 187
What's Good About the End / *Naomi Feigelson Chase* — 189
Why I Stayed / *Kay Marie Porterfield* — 199
Renaissance Summer / *Magi Stone* — 205

About the Authors — 207

Foreword

The authors in this wonderful anthology ask the very same questions of themselves that you might ask if you had the opportunity. They use their writing to try to figure out why what promised to be the best relationship in their lives turned out to be so destructive, so brutal, so devastating that it caused them mental anguish. Their emotional pain sometimes lasted longer than the time they spent in the relationship.

These authors creatively provide answers to the question which the title asks, sometimes with eloquent beauty, heartfelt sadness, familiar scenarios and even side-splitting humor. In some of the stories the pain is still fresh and palpable, the struggle with confusion feels, itself, a lot like the blows that caused it. Other women tell their no-less-sad tale with the benefit of greater emotional distance. From the punches of the batterer and the humiliation of the rapist, to the mind games of those who need total psychological control over another person, these stories bare the wounds of violence.

We have learned a great deal about violence against women in our society over the last two decades. It is now understood that power and control over women underlies men's use of violence. Until the mid 1970s domestic violence remained behind closed doors and battered women were not acknowledged. Today we estimate that one out of two women will be abused at some time in their lives.

Back then rape was defined only as forcible sexual intercourse and thought to be the almost exclusive province of the stranger on the street. Marital rape wasn't even a concept and date rape was attributed to the seductive woman's behavior. Statistics now tell us that one out of three women will be sexually assaulted and current rape laws acknowledge the variety of ways a woman can be forced into sex without her consent.

Child abuse wasn't a reportable offense in almost every state two decades ago and little girls' complaints of sexual abuse were passed off as fantasized love for daddy. Today statistics tell us that five percent of all children will be seriously physically abused and many more psychologically maltreated to the point that their proper development is threatened. Perhaps as many as one-third of all girls and one-fifth of all boys will be sexually abused before they reach 18 years old.

Sexual exploitation of women by those men in a trusted position — therapists, lawyers, doctors, priests — was unheard of twenty years ago. None of the women so victimized would have dared to think about their victimization much less write down the unspeakable deeds that were done to them. Currently many of these victims are winning large sums of money in civil personal injury law suits, a sort of war reparation remuneration. Most of them say it is the satisfaction of seeing the community condemn the man's behavior that is the most important to their healing.

In the not-so-distant past, if women who were victims of battering, emotional or sexual abuse had any angry feelings, their rage was usually reserved for themselves: What did they do to seduce him or to get the abuser so angry with them and how could they make the relationship better? Today women are beginning to ask different questions.

Reading the variety of tales told in this book through the stories, essays, and poems collected here, I was once again impressed with the infinite number of ways women are tortured by men with whom they are in a relationship. To be sure, women also do their share of torturing men, but there is a major difference. Even the mildest forms of psychological abuse perpetrated by men against women are augmented by what took place in the relationship or other relationships previously and by the threat of physical or sexual abuse in the future. Given women's statistical odds for being victimized, the very same act committed by a man against a woman takes on a different meaning in our culture than if it were committed by a woman against a man. This book provides the context for such an understanding of gendered abuse.

As I read the material collected here, I couldn't help but marvel at the strength of women's love for their men, no matter what those men did to them or to others. Even the women who knew they were being manipulated as it was occurring could not easily break that love bond. The women in this book loved the part of the batterer, the rapist, the con-artist or the little boy, who treated them well —

the part of him who loved her, initially setting the love bond into place. It is that part of him who listened to her concerns, responded to her feelings, validated her very being, made her body respond with quivering excitement, and dreamed her dreams, which kept his woman hooked on him.

The authors found themselves doing things they never dreamed they would be doing in order to keep intact whatever shreds of the relationship they were allowed to have. Through some of the worst, most degrading, most frightening abuse the love bond remained, weakening slowly, step by step. Usually a woman's cognitive functioning took over and with her rational being she terminated the relationship, understanding how toxic it was, but all the while her affective side still longed for his loving moments.

The fullest range of women's emotions are expressed by Kay Porterfield's authors. They laugh, cry, ridicule, show sarcasm, rage, sulk and feel a rush of competing feelings simultaneously. Sometimes they are maudlin and depressed, but they are also capable of great compassion and empathy. Their voices share every nuance of their descent into their own private hell and their slow climb out. With exquisite detail we hear ourselves falling in love and then having our hearts broken, again and again.

It is only when viewed together, story after story after story, that the individuality is stripped away so that the universality of the sad tale of male/female relationships is revealed. Women trained by years of sex-role stereotyped longing wait for their Prince Charming to appear. Then, when he comes, they give these Princes made-of-clay their hearts and souls, hoping for happiness forever after. When a little problem arises, they feel pain and hurt but quickly forgive their Prince, just like the fairy tale we have all heard tells them to do. He is grateful and rewards them with more love until the next transgression, followed again by loving contrition. So, the cycle goes on, with the pain and the hurt escalating until it takes over the good times. Yet those good memories live on, binding the woman to the man as if his hurtful behavior was an appendage that would simply drop off if only she could find the right answer.

Alas! The women in this book tell us the truth clearly. Although they desperately wish it would be different, they have learned that there is no magical right answer that can be supplied by the woman. The abusive man must learn the answer for himself. The woman who loved him can only go on with her own life. Here the courage of these women authors comes through. Eloquently they speak for every battered woman who has had to move on, wishing the good side would not have to end but understanding her own powerlessness to heal the man. These women move on, stronger, wiser, more courageous, and less likely to love another clay Prince who can break their hearts.

What's a nice girl like you doing in a relationship like this? Looking for love, of course.

Lenore E. A. Walker
August 30, 1991

Lenore Walker, is a licensed psychologist and nationally recognized expert on violence against women. Her books include *The Battered Woman*, a pioneering exploration of the Battered Woman's Syndrome, and *Terrifying Love*, which examines why battered women kill their abusers and how the courts respond. In addition to her private practice, she frequently testifies as an expert witness in court cases involving battered women. She is the founder and director of the Domestic Violence Institute, a research and policy-making organization. An adjunct professor of psychology at the University of Denver, she is also the president of the Psychology of Women Division of the American Psychological Association.

Introduction

Two years ago when I first put out the call for manuscripts which has resulted in *What's a Nice Girl Like You Doing In A Relationship Like This?*, I wasn't certain what would happen. I did know from my own involvement in and recovery from a physically and emotionally abusive marriage that although love doesn't have to hurt, sometimes it does, leaving deep wounds which take a great deal of time to heal.

As I wrote *Violent Voices*, a non-fiction book on domestic psychological terrorism, I learned a great deal from other women who had endured and survived relationships similar to my own. Ashamed to talk at first, they eventually opened up to share their stories and to ask if their romantic relationships might, by some slim chance, qualify as abusive. An artist told me about her boyfriend who never hit her, but who brutally kicked her dog and slashed her canvasses when he was angry. A counselor with a shelter for battered women said her fiancé was so jealous that he called her at least once an hour at work to make certain she wasn't seeing another man. A dentist detailed her life with a Sunday school teacher husband who recited Bible verses and called her a whore if she showed any pleasure during sex with him. As these women talked, I began to see a clear need for this anthology.

My goal in collecting material was two-fold. First, I hoped to raise awareness of the broad spectrum of violations women face and, too often, tolerate in the name of love. When we deepen our intimacy with another person, we paradoxically open ourselves to the potential for tremendous joy *and* tremendous heartache. Just as kind words and acts of kindness have the most impact when they come from a lover, so do cruel words and acts of cruelty.

All of us, women *and* men, at one time or another have been victims of romantic brutality. Although men have the edge on physical and sexual violence, women are just as capable of perpetrating mental cruelty, straight-jacket control tactics and infidelities as men. Given our cultural matrix, when women find ourselves victims of demeaning treatment at the hands of our lovers, we are slower than men to recognize what is happening to us. Once recognition sets in, we tend to more readily blame ourselves for a partner's behavior or to excuse away abuses of power as part of the price of love.

From the chronic erosion of constant put-downs to the one enormous and ugly violation which betrays trust and shakes our sense of self, domestic abuse can take many forms. According to the National Coalition Against Domestic Violence, battering, "is a pattern of behavior with the effects of establishing power and control over another person through fear and intimidation, often including the threat of use of violence." Not all domestic violence is physical. "Battering," continues the Coalition's position statement, "includes emotional abuse, economic abuse, sexual abuse, threats, using male privilege, intimidation, isolation and a variety of other behaviors used to maintain fear, intimidation and power." Until women become aware of what constitutes abusive behavior, we have little hope of facing up to our own situations or of changing them.

My second purpose in compiling a literary anthology was to explore the subject of domestic violence on a deeper level than I had been able to do when I wrote my non-fiction book. Short stories, poetry and personal essays have always been a critical part of my own healing process. They are a way to reach deeper truths and to approach the heart of painful issues in a more profound and moving way than straight exposition. By telling our stories or using them as the raw material for poetry and fiction, we writers transform our own lives and the lives of our readers. I hoped to pull together a collection of work that would be such a catalyst and would also reflect women's experience in a way a self-help book or a sociological study couldn't.

Unsure of the outcome, but trusting my muse, I placed ads in feminist and literary publications, asking for fiction, poetry and narrative essays dealing with chronic cruelty within the context of romantic relationships. My only taboos were against blame and self-pity. If this project was to be more than a he-done-me-wrong book, the women who wrote for it had to examine their own feelings. Their efforts needed to point the way toward healing from the cultural myths which draw us into damaging relationships and keep us there long after we know we should leave.

The response to my ads was overwhelming. Hundreds of manuscripts poured in. The works I received dealt with situations ranging from living with a cheating husband, loving a cold and emotionally distant man, being the other woman, loving an alcoholic man and finding oneself in the wicked step-mother role — to enduring rape and verbal and physical abuse. Whether sad, funny, angry, uppity, inspired, witty or filled with the joy which comes with healing, the majority were obviously based to some degree on personal experience.

Nearly every manuscript came with a letter. Many of those letters commented on my proposed title: *What's a Nice Girl Like You Doing In a Relationship Like This*? We were raised to be nice girls, my writers agreed, compliant little girls who lived to please other people at all costs and who weren't taught to set boundaries. Growing up in our party dresses and patent leather shoes, we learned that looking good on the outside was what mattered, so we cried on the inside and tried harder to make the people we loved happy with us. When we grew up, we became good women or good old gals, the adult versions of good little girls.

Codependency is the currently popular label for this type of behavior, but there is something rooted much deeper than codependency operating within women — a code of feminine behavior instilled from birth. The expectations placed on us about what it is to be girls, sugar and spice and everything nice, seem most difficult to transcend in love relationships. Yet they must be transcended if we are to attain authentic intimacy, to fully love and be loved. Although each writer phrased it differently, they wrote in chorus, "I used to be a nice girl. No more. I am my own woman now." That journey from nice girl to whole woman became the focus of this book.

Sifting through the manuscripts, I quickly discovered that choosing which ones to include was no easy task. All of the submissions in some way moved me, and I came away with a renewed faith in the community of women writers, their honesty and willingness to share their wisdom with others. Finally, when my house was filled with so much paper, my teenager started muttering about the fire hazard, I was forced to pick and choose.

The result is a gathering of women who express insights and emotions usually shared only with best friends over coffee those mornings when we sit at the kitchen table trying to figure out just what it is about cruel lovers that pulls us in the first place and why we settle even though we know we shouldn't. Our voices lower in hushed confessions of how we turn our rage on ourselves and of our hopes that next time it will be different, next time love won't hurt quite so much. To that end, we lend each other support and strength.

Confession is not only good for our personal psyches; it has a cleansing effect on the collective soul of society as well. Only by examining our wounds and giving name to them can we heal them. Jo Jane Pitt, whose short story is included in this volume, expresses the wishes of every woman involved in this project when she writes, "I hope that our experiences and articulation of them will strengthen, inspire and perhaps contribute in some way to a desperately needed shift in human consciousness that would actually heal and enrich the lives of men as well as women, and thus, children and whales and rain forests and oceans — for we are all interconnected in life on this planet."

LOVE SONG

When I think of you,
My breathing gets shallow;
Dark stars come out
And populate the night;
The Sun has trouble rising:
      I see its push against
      The resistant horizon,
And I know all is not well.

When I think of you,
Worms come out of their holes
And inch against dry sand;
The grass crouches lower
As if waiting for the blade;
And dogs bark in the distance
      For the last time.

When I think of you,
Tambourines stop playing;
And old women die
A day too soon;
And birthdays go unnoticed;
And fireflies lay eggs
      That hatch into birds
      That never fly away.

When I think of you,
The smells of Spring vanish;
And porcupines come to kiss,
Scratching my skin
      Right down to my soul;
The leaves on the trees
      Curl under,
As if before a storm
That will never end,
And will never be forgiven,
And will remind me always
Of you:
      Cold as the tombs,
      Evanescent as the sunset,
      Spoiling the night air
      With dying flowers
      And broken promises.

—Willa Koretz

growing pains

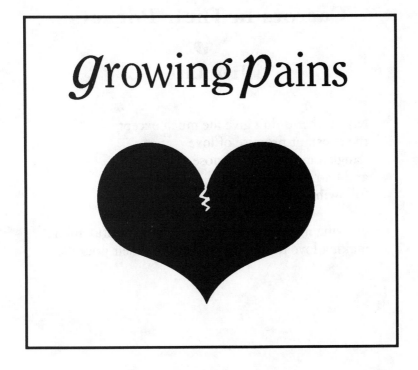

Carrots in Their Pockets

Iris Litt

My mother didn't give me much except
the constant promise of love
dangled in front of my nose
and I an eager little mule
following it through life

growing into a proud, sensitive and graceful animal
making love to men with carrots in their pockets.

The Night Before Father's Day

Denise Duhamel

The fireflies might have been bouncing balls in a sing-along.
You could have followed their luminous bellies, recited
the right lyrics, and lied so easily. It was night.
I wouldn't have believed you anyway, honest —
because of the raspberry liquor and the swaying candles.
It wasn't even your boat in which we were going to make love.
And I kept wondering if the flies, too, were for hire,
like passionate fireworks so far away from the shore.
It was a lie, a skit from *Love American Style,*
except you didn't love me at all

the night before Father's Day. I wasn't really young enough
to be your daughter, but it was close. You kidded
that you wanted a present because you had had four abortions,
four trips to the clinic with three different women.
I started to cry because of everything,
but mostly because you'd forgotten my birthday.
You said as though I had no right to my tears,
"Look, I never thought about you in that way at all,
You were just fun to have sex with.
You're a spunky girl, but honestly, you're not even my type."

It was like Christmas in an awful house
with no presents, just a blaring tv, and no one even trying
to sing a carol or make a turkey.
A voice in my head said, "You can fix this. You can fix this."
But was it my house or yours? It was a whole different
time, in a different part of the country.

A stronger voice in my head,
one that I usually only hear witnessing accidents
or getting a phone call about death,
said, "Get out. Get out for your life."

I looked through the porthole, Could I swim to shore?
What was lurking in the bay water? The dinghy
like a diaphram, elaborately tied up in knots, would take too long.
"I'm an old man, and I still look at each woman
I pass on the street. I wonder if she's wearing a bra
or the color of her pubic hair — I can't help it."
I was the child whose mind, in part, is off, far away.
Another part was stuck listening to a ranting parent.
You were unbuttoning your shirt like it was a turn-on,
regardless of me, regardless that I was planning my escape.

A Letter Refusing
the Inheritance

💔

Jo Jane Pitt

You. What the hell are you doing here. Haunting from my childhood. I don't even remember you, so long dead. Get away from me — you— you — *old grandaddy.* There is something else I must remember. Nothing to do with you.

> *It seemed to be simply another betrayal dream. In an old farmhouse similar to the one we moved into when first married, I searched from room to room for my husband, past bedrooms filled with beds full of people. On an enclosed side-porch, hidden they thought, were my husband and my friend. It seems the bed they were in was a single one, old-fashioned with a white iron headrail. I braced my feet against its spokes, and with body suspended, I pulled their hair. Then I saw through a shaded wire screen, lined on a porch rail, bottles and cans: dark brown slender-neck whiskey fifths, flat clear-glass gin pints, beer cans. Pow. There was a rifle shot. Cans and bottles, one by one, popped into midair explosions before the shatterings floated down. Pow. Powerless over alcohol. Pow. Powerless. Feet braced against the bed's white spokes, body suspended, I pulled their hair, and without a sound, I screamed.*

Now. You. Get away from me.
I'm sorry they all hated you. You were sick. I know that now. You weren't a sinner.
Though I don't remember much about you, uninvited, you form a surprisingly vivid image that I do not want.

Mama tells with amusement about our Sunday afternoon visits those days I was beginning to walk and talk, and how you would sit on the porch glider and shake your head and warn her, "She's too smart, that one. She'll be nothing but trouble."

Who the hell do you think you are to be so mean and ugly to me?

And you *are* ugly. I see your gray stubble beard and your slitted red-lined eyes, and those big rubber boots and baggy pants. You smell. Don't you touch me. Don't you come near me.

There you are sitting on the turned-over washtub by the pump house in Grannie's backyard. Everything was Grannie's, not yours. It was a dirt yard, swept clean with a rake every day in the summer by Grannie or Aunt Nora. Sometimes they let Darby and me help, but our scrapings never suited Grannie.

And I know about you getting up at five o'clock every morning to slink off behind the neighbor's cornfield bordered by a row of Grannie's forsythia and irises. Mama said you were too ashamed to stay around the house all day since you quit work and did not support your family.

You spent all day alone out in those woods hunting squirrels and rabbits. Mama says, "Hmph. He was mostly sitting on a stump where he kept his gin bottles hidden." Too ashamed to eat the food provided by the rest of the family, you made Grannie cook your squirrel or rabbit and you ate alone.

But Uncle Garland shared a reminiscence once, about which I remember nothing except cornbread and that it included you, incidentally, at supper. That puzzled me for it briefly interrupted an image of you hunched over a platter, alone at Grannie's kitchen table.

You showed me one time how to skin a rabbit. All I remember is your grin and the big knife in one movement from one end to the other slicing apart the fur.

Recently I ran into an old acquaintance at the grocery store. From only a few comments about the drinking and the separation, she recognized my situation. She told me that I am powerless over alcohol. And she said the alcoholic feels so much guilt that it's incomprehensible.

But you quit working, closed the store and garage, and it was the Depression, and you had three teenage children. Uncle Garland, all of his time outside school, worked a grown-man's day on that farm up the road that you leased; and my mother, just graduated, worked in the dimestore in town counting out jellybeans nine hours a day, six days a week. And a baby was growing inside Grannie just like the tumor twenty years later. Your children supported you. And one afternoon as she sat sewing a dress for home economics, you slapped Aunt Katie for not having a job like the others. She was fifteen years old.

As much as possible, I understand now. I knew all too well what my friend meant when she spoke of *family* illness.

But your children don't understand.

Neither does the child that I was, standing there in front of you. I saw your shrunken cheeks and scaly lips. You wore an old checkered cap like newsboys used to wear, shotgun propped against the washtub, holding up that dead squirrel in one hand, your mouth in a leer above your pointy chin, and a big shiny-blade knife in the other hand.

Remembering the sliced rabbit, I was about four years old then, fascinated, holding my breath at the sight of the little gray squirrel swinging empty-eyed from your hand.

Then you thrust it into my face.

Who the hell do you think you are, you—grandaddy, you— *Leave me alone.*

I did not summon you into my awake moments; I did not invite you into my dreams.

Even though they don't call it hate, your children all hated you so much that when I grew up I felt sorry for you. When the bars and the hard-drinking, lean, young men seemed like romance and fun, I felt sorry for you. In a family that turned out either saints or sinners, you were a sinner. Being no saint myself, I was left only the other choice. So I defended long-dead you. Especially because Mama seemed such a prude.

But mostly I forgot you.

No matter that my four memories of you are bad. I wouldn't think that an old drunk coot who was part of my life no more than five or six years had anything to do with me.

So who the hell are you to molest my dreams.

As you did the other night, in one brief moment in an exhausting, cluttered dream sequence. I am little. I am seven years old, in a short white cotton slip, barefoot. I am in the hayloft of a barn. You move toward me.

Between sleep and waking, I remembered that dream fragment, embarrassed that it sexually aroused me.

Fully awake I have no reason to believe that you ever did anything you shouldn't do to that child.

Still I deeply hated you.

And I remember: Grannie was keeping me while Mama and Daddy were at work. Darby of course already lived with you, born in that house like Uncle Garland. Aunt Katie's little boys from Tennessee were there, too. I see another cold gray day in the gray dirt yard. You were sitting on the wash tub, hands on knees, no rabbit or squirrel, oblivious to our games across the yard. We played house. I was the mother and Darby had to be the father even though he was shorter and a year younger than I. Baylen and Nate had to be our babies although Baylen who was about three-or-so was highly insulted and wanted to be father, also. We were at the part of the script where Nate was to pretend to disobey and I was to pretend-spank him with a little brittle forsythia switch I had broken off the bush the way Grannie did for real.

Baby saw the switch and ran from Mother. Mother, hollering, chased him. We ended in your spot.

You looked out of your huddled-over haze and yelled at me. You *damned* me. Called me a witch. The three little boys stayed behind me. Four children, natural allies, froze as if they had been playing sling the statue. You made me hand you the switch. You tapped it slowly against your open palm. Tap. You threatened. You went on, tap, and on, tap, and on.

I was hot and mad. And silent, standing before your curses.

So who the hell do you think you are. Get out of my bed.

Your bed, I remember, was one of those white iron ones with the curved head and footrail. After the Depression baby, Grannie gave you your own bed, Mama said. I know myself you smelled bad.

I don't have any memory of you actually touching me. But my daddy touched you.

I liked my daddy. He was quiet.

However, I don't remember him much either. He and Grannie— neither one outlived you by more than two or three years. Or my other grandfather. Or Baylen's and Nate's daddy, either.

According to Mama, my daddy got along with everybody — except Mama sometimes. And he liked you.

Mama said my daddy was a good old fellow, nonchalant, and never in a hurry. She used to get so mad on pretty, sunny Sunday afternoons. She'd be all dressed up still, from going to church with

Grannie, waiting for her date, my daddy, to come for their drive. You'd be sitting on the green metal front porch glider that outlasted you and Daddy and Grannie. Grannie's tulips and daffodils planted in a circle around the big oak in the front yard must have sent out bright sparks of red and yellow, the way they looked years later when the boys and I hid Easter eggs in them. The front yard grass was probably turning green. The twisted sour-apple tree at the end of the porch that held Darby's swing, also years later, must have worn its pink blossoms. And you'd talk Daddy into a game of checkers when he came up. There my mama would be rocking with the women, while the row of crepe myrtles with their clusters of hot pink petals sent longer and longer shadows across the jutted drive. She'd be rocking and patting her foot, she said, while you and Daddy played checkers on until supper time.

I recall that my daddy, like you, enjoyed eating squirrel and other strange foods like "chitlins" and oysters. He also liked to step out to the smokehouse with his brothers down at his daddy's farm where they passed around whiskey. Sometimes it was like water inside a widemouthed jar; sometimes it was in a bottle inside a paper sack. For me, the smokehouse with the men was more exciting than the front porch with the women rocking. It was a blend of daddy smells: of Old Spice aftershave, and Lucky Strikes, and my fat uncle's cigar and whiskey and country hams curing.

I guess that is why it isn't strange that my daddy's the only person I ever saw touch you. That early Saturday morning, he drove me from town to Grannie's to stay while Mama worked. He was going to drop me off as always until Grannie, with Darby hanging onto the skirt of her cotton print dress, rushed out to the porch. It was sunny and seemed like it was spring with that dew-filled cool that promises hot by ten o'clock. Grannie's flowers were budding. She told Daddy that you hadn't got up yet. Everybody knew you were always up by five to go hunting. She couldn't wake you and Uncle Garland had already gone to town to his shop. She was worried.

She waited with Aunt Nora and Darby, staying back at the door. But when Daddy stepped into the bedroom I was right under him, of course, and darted past him and stood right at the foot of your bed.

Your teeth were out so your jaws were more shrunken than usual with little blue and red veins traced all over your thin skin, your pointy nose sticking up, gums red inside your open mouth.

Your face was coated with a gray beard, and each breath sent out a rattle with a snort at the end. You were ugly. I was quiet and still, way back inside myself somewhere, looking out. Daddy called you several times, loudly, and shook you and touched you and you didn't answer. He leaned over and put his finger on your eyelid and forced it open. Then your eyeball rolled up and there was nothing but white with red streaks. Slowly, he closed the lid. Then he looked around at Grannie.

When the ambulance came to take you to the hospital in town, Darby and I stood on the porch and watched the attendants, with you on the skinny bed on wheels, put you into it. You vanished and I don't think I much noticed.

It was on that bed in Grannie's room that Daddy rested, that Christmas I was nine. Grannie lay in her bed crosswise the other end of the room. They had told me she was dying. But Mama told me only that my daddy was sick. So when he slept through the Christmas Eve gift opening, and I burst into the cool, dark, bedroom with its linoleum rug and frosty windowpanes, I tried to wake him to show him my presents, he grunted and didn't really answer and suddenly Mama's fingers pinched into my arm and yanked me out of there.

I never thought before how that was the same bed. Your bed. And then it was only eleven days later I stood at the end of my daddy's bed in our own house, looking out from that place I had found way back inside of me. And I stood alone on our front porch and watched the ambulance people wheel Daddy away under a white sheet, past me. I did not even remember you that day. They buried Grannie three weeks later.

Mama said you must not have always been a *disappointment.* She would not say the word drunk because that did not sound nice.

But I know now about *denial.*

The one nice thing, though, that I ever knew about you came surprisingly from Mama. You were a very handsome young man, weren't you? Mama's photograph album verifies it: a straight, lean, taut-muscled, dark-haired fellow, with bright round eyes, high cheekbones, in one of those bathing suits with a top like an undershirt and tight trunks down to your knees. You are smiling and posing in front of a backdrop of painted palm trees. I notice now that you resemble my ex-husband.

But it is terrible enough without you who have nothing to do with me, coming back at this time when my marriage has fallen apart. In those days and nights of the final countdown, he was so sick with drinking and drugs, he rarely came home anymore. When he did, it was with abusive curses, my tears and threats, our nervous and frightened children hanging back, watching.

You have nothing to do with me, old grandaddy.

You—who Mama said was once young and dashing. Grannie was the eldest daughter of a "Primptive" Baptist preacher. She was sweet-sixteen and you were twenty-two when you met her. You gave her a gold bracelet for an engagement token because everyone thought she was too young for a ring, and Mama said Grannie mentioned something about some poetry you wrote for her.

You goddamn dirty old gin-breathed, scratchy-faced bastard. *You wrote poetry?*

Well, where the hell is it now.

And who cares anyway.

Since the dream of you, I remember my husband before he left. He would snarl *bitch* and pass out, his dentures not only out of his mouth but split down the middle. They broke once when they fell out one two-thirty a.m., as he vomited all over himself and the side of the car. I groped along a quarter of mile of road-shoulder until I found them.

Next to me in bed, this man was almost toothless from neglect — not age; his unshaven cheeks sunk in, his breath rattled and snorted. He was killing himself one day at a time. And he smelled bad. Granddaddy, I am sorry nobody loved you and they all believe you were a no-good sinner when you were really sick and there was no one to help.

But I want you out of my head, my bed, my dreams.
Who the hell do you think you are?

Tree Rings

♥

Donna Decker

In a flash, I see
the red tile floor,
my sister and me on the red-chipped stairs,
holding tight to the pine bannister bars,
while he mopped up the floor with Mother,

and wouldn't let me run to the corner
for Grandpa whose mahogany rifle
would have smoked
as it shouted to the sky for rain,
the pitch boom of its thunder
wrenching him off her back.

Flash, I'm Superman,
freezing his next blow with my breath.
I'm God's Angel,
and command him to lay down his steel.
I am the Good Witch;
when I blink he is a coat-tree,
a pint-sized sculpture of a man.
I am Zeus, splitting open the sky,
commanding Zephyr to purse his lips
and blow him to the river
where he is killi, minnow,
dodging dinner-angling droop-mouthed carp,

so I am not trapped on those bleeding stairs
with Helen,

crash of milk bottles,
the roar of a woman breaking
in front of her children,
his voice descending like a dark net,
to catch me over twenty years later
as I try to work my feet.

Flash — I'm in my old lover's
small white meditation room.
In a mute liquor-netted bull rage,
he shoves.
My head bounces like a coconut
on the shiny pine floor.
When I think — this is love —
he shakes me till I know
my neck will snap like a green bean,
my soul, the small pea,
rolling across the wood.

Flash—I am back in our bed.
Like a summer shower,
your love dares to rain.
But I am braced like the last pine
for lightening,
and, for now, the cool drops fall on wood.

Hooks

💔

Karen Bowden

He calls me a fake
as he carefully chooses
the china he'll break.

Fuck off he shouts
and in the hollow of that sound
I whisper I've been doing just that
since my brother

and he sneers
it might be worth
two rooms of broken china
if I had no brother.

       The children stopped.
       They had what they wanted.
       A boy

       my brother - clumsy
       and afraid of worms.

       I understood worms
       and threading hooks

       so I threaded his hook
       while our father watched

I faked it
beat him at marbles
threw a ball farther.

When my father died
my skin wept
from every pore
while my brother's mouth twisted.

Now my mouth curls
around the broken china
he doesn't care about.

I smash the one dish that matters

his grandmother's bowl

and he laughs
caught.

Jessie

💔

Elspeth Cameron Ritchie

Jessie walked though the tall weeds along the river. Two black cats and one striped, trailed behind. Breaking through to the beach, she hopped down to the seaweed-strewn sand. She pulled from her bag three items: a bottle, a doll and a candle.

It was noisy there in the dark under the stars. Waves slapped at her feet. Across the cove a boat sputtered, red and green lights glowing. A helicopter beat at the night sky.

Her anger lay like a tide, ebbing and rising with her thoughts. But the air was still, and so she was able to light the candle. It glowed on the doll, revealing a clay woman, with snakes in her hair and on her lap. One of the black cats bounded to Jessie's feet, meowing for a caress.

She smiled, then thought of her last kiss with Don and frowned. It had been on this beach, where the Patuxent lapped toward the Chesapeake Bay, although that night the full moon shone. Baby spot had been flipping in the air, flashing silver, six inches off shore. She and Don slipped off their clothes, and played in the shallow water, until he, gasping at a jellyfish sting, had run for the beach. She had strode in nude, expecting him to grab at her buttocks. She had wanted him to stroke her breasts, as he had the weekend before.

Instead he said, "We have to talk."

"Okay," she said, wondering why he had to ruin it.

"Jessie, you're very nice, but..."

"But?" she said, knowing.

"Jessie, I like you, but well, I'm not that attracted to you. If you could lose some weight...and you are drinking too much. People at the office are starting to suspect."

"Suspect what, you bastard?" she had thought. She wanted to

hit him, but nice girls from Farmington didn't hit young men (even if they were now thirty-two). Besides, she *wasn't* fat. Sure she could lose a few pounds, but then, so could he. Suddenly the cold duck they'd been drinking had lost its sparkle. The evening fizzled into separate bedrooms. She didn't weep until she was alone.

After that, work was tense because she had to see him. She'd spied him pinching the new secretary, but couldn't do anything about it. But tonight, tonight was her night to get back at him.

She opened the bottle of blush Chablis, her second, that night, first pouring a little on the sand, for the sea god Poseidon, then drinking two long swallows. Clouds started to obscure the stars.

She must work fast. She started to sing a Credence Clearwater song. "I see a bad moon arising. I see trouble coming soon." Gathering the driftwood into a pile, she added gas she'd siphoned earlier from the rototiller.

Many years ago she'd learned the fundamentals of witchcraft and had expanded on those basics to develop her own unique style. But until now she had only used it to help grow tomatoes. She'd raised the most productive yellow tomato plants in the county, and brought great salads of tomatoes and basil to company picnics. If her co-workers only had known of the mice carcasses added to the fertilizer.

This ceremony tonight was the first act of vengeance she had done, but her mother had practiced retaliation against her stepfather for many years. Mom hadn't used witchcraft, but the times Jessie's stepfather had hit her mother, when Jessie was eleven, had been repaid with eight years of headaches and martyrdom. Jessie, herself, had never repaid her stepfather for his fondling of her. Until now, she'd been above that.

She didn't mind it at first. At first, she loved it when "Uncle John," as she was supposed to call him, had hugged her. His lap was wide. Soon though, the stiffness alarmed her. She mentioned it once to her mother, who shrieked, "You slut!" and headed for her with her beer bottle.

That was before the second divorce. Later she had learned to avoid both her mother and her mother's boyfriends. Eating, and getting fat had helped. No lasting relationships with men, although she thankfully gave up her virginity at sixteen. She had never thought herself in love until she fell for the man who had jilted her last weekend. So much for loving men.

Cats rubbed her feet as she lit the driftwood. Another swig

from the bottle. She lit a Marlboro Light. Funny, how she had been so against smoking, on the nights when her mother burned the chaise lounge. Now she too drank, ate ice cream ravenously, vomited and smoked. It partially helped.

The gas flamed blue, scampering over the salt-seasoned driftwood. She threw on some dry brambles. The fire began to catch, tentatively licking up towards the roots of locust trees.

She had done so much for Don, she thought bitterly. Fed him pesto, taught him windsurfing, introduced him to her boss when he was out of a job. Now he was bounding up the career ladder, while she, as a woman, was still asked to type. But only by those who did not know better.

White smoke began to plume upwards, amid the scraggled oak limbs. She sprinkled powder from her bag, shavings of cedar berries, crab shells, coriander seeds and fawn bones, all gathered from the adjoining Southern Maryland acres.

Jessie seated herself on a grass tuffet. Two more swallows and another light. Faintly she heard the telephone from the house ringing. It might be him — but probably was her mother, three sheets to the wind. "Why don't you call? When are you going to give me a grandson? Why don't you finish college?" No apologies for having missed her birthday again.

Smells gathered in the August air. She stood up, removed her shirt, and then her shorts. Clad only in her bikini bottoms, she strode into the shallow river, kicking up phosphorescent sea. Translucent spineless sea pumpkins switched on as they bounced against her bare legs. No jellyfish tonight.

Should she attempt to kill him or not? The thought had been racing through her head since Sunday. If not here, where? She could lure him down to the beach, feed him wine, push his head down into the shallow waters, let her anger peak and then flow.

Murder. Could she, should she do it? Her rage blew through her. But nice girls did not kill. Maybe she should confine her efforts to his essence. If her clay doll killed, she would not be sent to prison. Medusa would go.

Out from the bag came Don. His hair, his shaving cream, a cheap plastic bag containing his semen she'd soaked from where it had dried on her sheet. She added sand, mud, cigarette ashes and oyster shells, crudely shaped his head and genitals. He looked weak then, a mere plaything.

Holding the mass in her hand, almost naked, wood burning

red, she stood over the fire. Should I kill?

She had nearly killed her stepfather, Uncle John, that last time. He had broken into her room, tearing open the cheap drywall. An antique letter opener was all she had, but when he'd clasped her thighs, she'd raised it. When she paused for an instant before plunging it into him, he looked up, saw the blade, and he had pivoted and dashed her on the floor. But he left then. He had divorced her mother soon after. She never saw "Uncle John" again.

Three questions: should she throw his fluids in? Would he die? If he didn't perish from the fire, should she slay him otherwise?

"Don, Don, John. Feel my power Don. Don! John!" She swung the bag containing his image high, then stopped reflecting. Would just killing him help? She needed to take his power first.

Medusa would do it. Unraveling one of the snakes on the clay doll's lap, Jessie thrust it once, twice, three times into the soft bag until the bag's contents spilled into the roaring cedar-scented flames. There, now, Medusa had sapped his power, killed him the way her mother had killed her real father.

The previously suppressed memory suddenly tore at Jessie so fiercely, she sat down hard on the beach. It was in the kitchen. Jessie was eating applesauce for lunch. She must have been two or so, long before starting kindergarten. Her father came in. He had been gone, a lot. Her mother was angry; Jess knew that Mom had been mad for weeks. She would forget to feed her or else stuff food in her mouth when she was angry. Jess was afraid of Mom when she was like this. Last time Mom had burned her. Tommy was crying in the other room. Tommy always cried.

Dad was quiet, too quiet. He smelled. Then as Mom continued to yell, he got up from where he was sitting. To little Jessie he seemed like a giant. He spilled an oil lamp as he towered up, silently raging. He grabbed, not Mom, but Jessie. Yanking her from her high chair, he shouted at Mom, "We're leaving, you bitch! The doctor said those cigarette burns on her leg were from you. You're crazy!"

"Crazy? You're the drunk! Take her and I'll kill you!"

"Try it, whore!" He strode toward the door with Jess. "I'll be back for Tommy!"

Mom moved fast. Grabbing an old knife from the stove, she lunged. The rusty steel gouged through his shirt, entering his side. He stopped, surprised. Gently, slowly setting Jessie down, he ebbed to the floor. The blood puddle grew.

So did the flames from the oil lamp he had knocked down. They lapped on her fallen bib, tongued upwards to the yellow curtains. Jessie, fallen out the kitchen door, saw her mother run inward towards Tommy's crib. Her father reached out toward her, lying in the sill. "Jessie, help me!"

But she froze. Her legs didn't work.

"Jess!"

Suddenly the kitchen seemed to tide in flames. The cooking oil and bacon grease on the stove caught. It was then that her mother erupted out the door with her baby brother. Mom tripped over Dad, who clutched at her leg, but Mom pulled away and kept running. Suddenly able to move, Jessie turned her back on her father and followed her mother.

"Jess, Jess, please help me! Call for help, Jessie!" he begged.

Now years later on the starlit sand, Jessie shuddered, heaved. Why hadn't she remembered that before? The official version was that her father had passed out drunk, a cigarette had caught and the trailer was consumed in flames. But this memory was too vivid to be imagination.

Mom had killed Dad.

She, Jessie, couldn't kill Don, not really. He didn't deserve to die.

Who did? Mom, Dad or Jessie? Maybe Jessie did. Should she go die in these phosphorescent waters? Forget what had just torn upward through her memory. Would that appease the vengeful gods? She swigged at the bottle, spilling wine onto the sand. Maybe dying would ease the pain. There was a knife in the kitchen. She could always use that on herself.

From behind her came a demanding meow. The striped cat rubbed her back. One black cat jumped on her lap, tilting the clay doll into the sand. His black brother cried from the beach. The fire was getting too large. A spark landed in the dry reeds and caught.

Jessie leapt up hastily. She wasn't planning to burn down the beach. And she hadn't fed the cats. She used her abandoned shirt to throw river water on the sparks which had caught, and then on the fire itself. It settled down to a comfortable level. Kicking sand over the flames, she added the rest of her wine to drown the fire. When it was almost extinguished, she threw Medusa in to undo the spell, and went back to the house. The cats followed.

Why I Am Wanting to Solve Every Echo Because

♥

Beverly G. Merrick

Grandfather, the fisherman
    did not think to make me a fisherwoman,
Grandmother, the hotel cook
    did not think to call herself a chef.

Father, the war-time soldier
    is a gentleman.
Mother, the piece-time welder
    is not a gentle woman.

Son, who sees himself a future poet
    painfully flexes his muscles.
Daughter, who sees herself a future president
    slopes her shoulders, hides her breasts.

The male minister, a word merchant
    is God's disciple
The female teacher, God's messenger
    is a word merchant.

The players, who tackle in the mud
    see only the game, cannot hear the spectators.
The spectators, who cannot play in the game
    see only the mud, can only speculate.

The words, "We the people," mean we the men.
The echoes, "Me Too," mean we the women. . .

and because so many are deaf to those echoes
and because so many hear, but deny there are echoes
and because so many just say

SHUT UP!

dark enchantments

Null and Void

💔

Fabian Worsham

I have been watching
the woman next door
as daily she mourns
the husband she lives with
but cannot love,
the lover she wants
who wants her no longer.
Each morning she rises
to coffee and laundry,
the coffee is only coffee;
the damp sheet stuffed
in the drier will never again
be a white sail strung
from a bamboo mast
or a picnic cloth
flapping on the sand.
She's beyond pretending,
beyond dreaming of worlds
that vanished with her affection
for each man, the husband
she turns her back to,
the lover who turned his back,
walked up the hill
and out of sight.
After years invested
in dreams of love, she wakes
each day to the poverty
of her ranch-style home,

her husband bald and indebted.
I want to tell this woman
that only now is she free
to become her own lover,
but she would not believe me.
For her, that one man's hand
gentle against her cheek
was the only convincing thing.

The Astounding Capabilities
of the Human Mind

💔

Candice Rowe

The human brain weighs just under three pounds and is roughly the size of two clenched fists held tightly together. Doctors can probe the brain with electric prods and the patient can see someone long dead, can hear some sound from long ago, or can recall events long forgotten. The mind can supply continuity to a dashed line and can make sense of chaos.

To wit: Photos of an ensemble of comedians appearing at a popular downtown hotspot have been printed recently in newspapers and magazines. Upon angling the page just so, I see that one of these men resembles him.

In one picture he has on a hat with a mock mercury vapor lamp, attached miner's fashion. His head is turned in three-quarter manner toward the viewer, one of his eyebrows taking a deep dip to indicate his superiority and disdain. His attitude belies any notion of intellectuality, emphasizing rather, as academicians put it, a person athletically gifted. The young man in the picture has the same white blonde hair (from what is visible under the miner's hat) and the same pale eyes that take on color under the influence of some emotion, throwing back light like bottlecaps catching the sun. The mind can make him walk, arms stiffly at sides, torso bent forward, tacking along. The mind can make him speak, the voice full of static, jittery, the laugh of an axe maniac or a boy who's done something very wrong and been caught but wants to maintain his dignity in a difficult situation.

After this discovery it's easier to spot look-alikes in crowds, in dreams, and even in Ford pickups, six cylinder, as the driver's arm is hanging out the window and the bill of his baseball cap is pulled down over his head. He is also in movie crowd shots, moving briskly away on busy streets. And sometimes he is in the face of the lousy guys who've played out their options and sit in dark barrooms on June mornings sucking on beer bottles while they try to put their fingers on the one cancer cell, the one bad break, the one word or look that propelled them forever through the grille-windowed door and keeps them nailed to the scarred wooden bar.

Okay. This is what they've told me. He went to a football celebration party and drank too much. There was a girl there, much too young. He said he would take her home and he did. But not before he raped her. Two times. Under oath he said he drank with her, but he never touched her. But he is the worst liar in the world. These are some of the lies he has told me: "My mother is my stepmother." She is his real mother. She has, from what I've seen over the counter of Swedlum's Home Bakery where she decorates cakes for all occasions, the same pale eyes and hair and the same small nose reminiscent of a carnival prize toy. "My sister is a Combat Zone hooker." His sister is a hairstylist at A Cut Above Salon. "I get thirty dollars an hour as a steel worker." He had no steady job. Sometimes his friends let him drive a lumber truck, but once he put some pine planks through a guy's open Subaru window, narrowly missing a tot in a safety seat.

It was easy to tell when he was lying. He'd look out as though he were viewing a wide Montana horizon and his eyes would go clear and then they'd take on a blueness like dark ice forming.

For this transgression he got five to eight years of hard time. They tell me also a bunch of concurrents...kidnapping, assault and battery. They talk about AIDS and dehumanization, of a life shot to hell in about twenty minutes on a cold January morning. And someone whose voice sounds pretty much like mine asks, "And what am I supposed to do now?" The human spirit endures, someone blathers. And to that I say, Bangtail the human spirit.

Bangtail the human brain too, with its cell upon cell hivelike each one with his image on into perpetuity.

The mind is also capable of numbing hindsight. Now it says quite cockily: Never trust a young man you meet under the hood of a '76 Plymouth that has a busted fanbelt and a frozen-up alternator after both of you come along and offer to aid the frazzled grandmother who has broken down on Route 128 (Silcon Highway East) and whose terrible grandsons fire rotten pignuts off the rusted hulk the entire time the two of you are under that hood tacking together an emergency fanbelt that will hold only long enough for the grandmother to drive to the nearest exit and turn off into a gas station. Further: Never trust a liar. Never trust a man who doesn't own a watch. Never trust a man who starts his car with a screwdriver. Never trust a man who kisses with his eyes wide open. He claimed: "I like to keep in touch that way." You think: His eyes are like pinpoints of stars spinning away or even tiny knifepoints of light.

But all that is now.

Now too there are the prison treatises. Skipping the Marxist dribble, the shattering of God's image, the brutality of guards...these themes run like the marbling of fat through a side of beef...one finds the things that ease the clenching of the heart.

Those inmates who are not strung out on heroin or other illegal substances, those who are not studying law and planning their appeals, those who are not writing lengthy diatribes on prison reform or their Life-And-Hard-Times books, those who still have a brainstem and something springing from it, are attempting to communicate telepathically with those on the outside.

Imagine these thoughts, coddled, nurtured, self-important, sidewinding, catapulting, vortexing through the ether willy-nilly; what's the chance of their landing in the wheelhouse? The universe is, after all, haphazardly run at best.

The last time I saw him, we had a locked screen door between us. He wore a Celtic green shirt that made his face too pink. He pressed up against the frame and told me, "Open the door." I could feel the warmth of his body, could see how his face was taking on a pained look. His hand spread out over the rusty mesh of the screening and I wanted more than anything to step forward and press my hand against his, to kiss him through the metal where at least we'd have that for safety.

Then he was gone. Down the stairs, yelling back over his shoulder, "Fuck you." And then, seeing how he doesn't like things to end on a sour note, ever, he called from the sidewalk, "I hope this doesn't spoil our friendship."

I hate that word "friend" between us. It's reminiscent of fiery or fiend. For those who cut near the bone. For those who stare down silent white corridors and are not afraid to make noise or dirty handprints on the perfect walls. For those who manage to outscream the wind and outpace the thing waiting around corners. For them, the word friend is an outrage in a sacred place.

Again, without bidding, the heart is ready to tow the line, leap the chasm. It supplies, without warning, to the palm of the hand the sloping contours of his naked back. The muscles, or the tactile memory thereof, rise up, softly, gently, much in the way things drowned rise to the surface in a body of still water.

But for all the amazing things the brain can do, it has no capacity for regeneration.

To wit: Someone has taken the time and care to repeatedly call my answering machine leaving the following messages: First the fuzzy, high-pitched whine that leads into strangulated mechanical sounds and the line going dead. Then a message that begins in the same fashion and progresses to a warbly voice — I am reminded of those 78 Disney records of singing crickets and winsome princesses, their voices high-pitched and tinny, yet wrenchingly sweet — uttering "I still dream of you." The following call is the best. The message starts a few notes before the lyrics kick in. The voice sings: "If I still dream of you, how come I can't hold you in my arms?" The voice stammers, finds strength and warbles on in true country western love-your-man-come-hell-or-high-water-style. "I still miss you," the voice sings sadly, the last refrain cut short, reminding one of how a person might be snatched off in a hurricane or tornado or some other natural disaster. It's hard not to cry at the tinned up-sadness.

Is all this the work of some random prankster idling away the dull morning hours? Some ex-child cryptographer? (We all had those secret decoder rings from our breakfast cereal boxes and we all believed we had the edge on the Russkies with our ciphering skills.) Or maybe the desperate attempts of someone held incommunicado, someone who needs to affirm the reception of his telepathic messages?

Even through the electronic gadgetry I imagine his breathing as he works his recorder to allow the words their exodus to my machine.

This is not a tale of descent into hell. Sure, friends and family are concerned. I have, on occasion, refused to leave the house, waiting for his next message. And it comes: "Sometimes it's hard to be a woman, giving all your love to just one man."

Sure I believe it's him, against all probabilities that they would allow him out of his cell and provide him with access to a phone, not to mention a recording device, a Tammy Wynette tape — is that all convicts listen to, country and western bad times for the heart music? — as well as enough dimes to make frequent phone calls?

But to the mind these are minor nuisances. And to a mind throttle open, full tilt, these obstacles are not even worth considering.

The mind also enjoys a bit of humor at the heart's expense. It says, out loud to a room full of people, "So he made one little fucking mistake."

Sometimes the whole thing is like a stain spreading and setting in. Soon there are strange cars parked outside my house at all hours of the night. These are old cars, wide-bodied with up-swept tail fins that put me in mind of predatory animals. Upon studying these cars, I can see the tiny muzzle flash of cigarette lighter. And sometimes, the bobbing of a tiny flame. Exactly one hour after the sighting, the car moves the wrong way up the street and disappears.

The mind here is called up to adduce, induce, deduce, and reduce. If it continues on its present track, what follows will delineate the clichéd fall into madness. If it grabs itself by the hackles, digs in its heels, and arrests the slide, then there's hope.

The brain is truly an incredible organ.

The following morning it notes with startling clarity the strength of the breeze clipping in from Canada, the way it cuts through the interstices in a wool sweater. All it needs, frankly, is a distraction.

So by noon, the mind no longer directs the body to call home and check for musical messages. The stomach speaks a tune also. How long does one serve a five-to-eight with a bunch of concurrents and a filed charge, kidnapping, held in lieu of good or bad behavior? And bangtail it, the most rational of minds knows by now he's in more trouble, so the stomach orders up quite a lunch: macaroni and cheese, bread buttered to the hilt, treats from the dessert wagon. Because how old will I be when he gets out, thirty-eight?

By evening the mind is convinced, hell, no, it knows, we'll never see him again. There is no one watching from a car parked outside the house. No one is following me to the post office or corner store. No one is making calls because one of them, perhaps I forgot to mention this, comes at 2 a.m. The male voice says, "Please don't hang up. Talk to me. I'm an admirer of yours." I hold my hand over the receiver the ultimate talker, not wanting to give this mystery man even a shakey breath of mine for free. We know this is not him because he never says please.

The mind, a blackboard wiped clean; metal filings rendered meaningless on a magnetic tape, decrees the following: No more men arriving at night in prison denims. We have ordered from central casting these particular fantasies, models of him that are slim and grayed — he will be twenty-nine when he gets out and worldly-wise and ready for the love of a good woman. Another model, ruggedly muscular from the prison gym and smoldering with societal resentments, kidnaps the poor woman, taking her to a furnished cabin in the Berkshires. These fantasies are well-ordered as I have on the ready a bag holding clothes that don't make me look fat, enough hair goop to style for a week, birth control devices, et cetera. And I'm always kidnapped on my vacation so I won't miss work and get fired.

The most recent innovation is the ex-con who arrives and surprises me as I am coming home from work carrying freshly cut flowers. This ex-con is overdressed and has too many gold neck chains. He takes me to a Japanese steak house in his flashy car (American, overpriced, crushed velour interior that holds your imprint long after you've departed) where he over-orders and tries hard to be sophisticated, but presently I guess he has taken to dealing drugs and I am morally outraged. Perhaps this last creation is the harbinger from the mind that an emotional separation from these fantasies is in order.

No more of these men, any model. This is difficult. I've grown accustomed to their ways with me. But the mind can wipe out emotional attachments quicker than a chalk drawing on a rainy sidewalk. The mind clears its screens and readies its lasers.

This morning in the weak early light, my teeth appear translucent. My tongue moves visibly behind them. Too, they are the color of gray/purple mussel shells.

The scrambling mind poises on the edge of the abyss and looks in with a rational eye toward salvation. Wait up, it says. If we keep up with this, we're circling the drain. If we pull out now, we can minimize damages. We can still reconnoiter, rationalize, extemporize. We've passed a night without him. There's hope.

The mind has this capacity also: to wrest a new truth from an old truth, rendering the latter an untruth.

So by the second day of this new plan, after a night spent peacefully, the fair-haired cons replaced by Mexicans with shining white teeth like tiny strong animals, these men back to back like dominoes, and all dressed in fringed boleros and sombreros, putting me in mind of a reconditioned '64 Chevy — by this second day, the mind is reconciled...no, better than reconciled, it has made something of the tatters, but there's still some impulse of resistance.

So the mind states unequivocally that (1) she is too old to wait for him. Wait for what it asks. For the two-thirds of that five-to-eight year sentence? (2) He's a con now, a jailbird, a scofflaw. She's an educated reasonable professional. (3) Besides, how can she know with any surety he'll even remember her? But logic is short-circuited here. Would you remember a woman who said to you, as you lay naked above her, you eating a piece of chocolate, she says to you, "See if you can drop that into my mouth from that height and if you miss, you owe lunch." Then you owed her lunch. Or this. She insists you make love to her on her front porch, but because of the city's stupid crime lights everything has a jaundiced look, and it's springtime so it's chilly and her neighbor is a wicked busybody and you've got this sort of hang up from the charges hanging over your head that you've avoided telling her about (the rape, two counts), so you say, "I don't like doing stuff outside." But she leans into you and puts the tip of her tongue on your nose that she claims looks like a stuffed animal's and runs it lightly over that channel under the nose leading to the lips. (Christ, she'd even know the name of it, if you asked her.) (Philtrum, she thinks smugly.) So you do it outside on the porch anyhow.

Okay. So he'd probably remember her.

But the wait for him involves that little sidetrip over the edge, so we opt for the contingency plan. Forget him. He doesn't call every Friday morning at ten or send emissaries in old model cars to stake out the house. There are not thoughts wending their way through the ether.

And the mind would be happy with all this, copacetic, contented, if it were not for that bangtail little worm of the heart, usurping power from some inconspicuous groove in the walnut-like convolutions of the brain where the doctor's probe can't even find it. That thing keeps slugging like a badger, reminding her of how men are cowards, afraid of the black hall of love, while women don't feel right until they're hopelessly lost in its labyrinthine corridors again. And how the only way she'll ever be really free of him, cleaned free of him, exorcised and retempered, the only way would be to blast that mind to the moon, that repository for all things lost.

Disappeared

♥

Barbara Foster

Did you get hit by a car,
Or fall into a sewer?
Did amnesia cause you
To forget our pledges
Easy as shirts left
At a Chinese laundry?

Shall I call "Missing Persons"
Describe your nefarious kisses?
If they solve the mystery
I'll pay my reward
In tidal waves of tears

I'll charge you with criminal
    neglect
Bear witness to your guilt
The sentence will be heinous
Since you don't care
The penalty falls on
    my neck
Sharp as the guillotine's
    blade.

In Six Short Lessons

♥

Cris Mazza

Week #1

1. Meet Class

Who says meeting new people is difficult. Plenty of people will always need dog-training classes. Twenty students per class, four classes per week, roughly six sessions a year, that's 480 new people I've met this year. I would tell them about it in divorce therapy group, if I were still going — what a hostile crowd, glad I never opened my mouth.

2. Introduce cardinal rule #1: Never accept undesirable behavior. Always reward only desirable behavior. Be 100% consistent.

I'll have to tell them what happens when undesirable behavior is rewarded even if unintentionally. I have to give an example. The illustration I always use is when you attempt to get a dog to let go of a sock he's been chewing by trying to pull it out of his mouth: Dogs love tug-o'-war; you're giving him a great time; his favorite reward is a great time; so you've taught him to never let you have anything he's got because you've been rewarding him for hanging onto it. One time I had enough courage to tell Derek I was going to use him as an example of this. Luckily he decided not to listen so I didn't elaborate. I could imagine it, though, calmly telling them that Derek thoroughly enjoyed each sweaty, aching, sometimes bloody, shattering moment — especially if I was fighting back, he loved it more. Maybe in a way I was being rewarded too: a dumpy girl like me with a guy like him? It should've been the same as every other time I've walked past a construction site. Someone (this time Derek) shouts, "Hey, my friend here says you got nothing to offer!" Except this time I smiled at him. He looked so much like those advertisements where a job in a generic form of manual labor looks like a romantic, patriotic, religious experience: silhouetted guys in slow motion with showers of sparks behind them. He didn't have a pot gut, his hair was clean, his teeth were all there, his jeans fit, it was just about sunset. Halfway on my way to becoming a feminist lawyer and wound up married to an illiterate laborer. As though all the cardinal rules ceased to exist. Quit school when my nose was broken. His forehead in the dark. Didn't he say it was an accident? But he also took the closet door off its hinges, his voice coming from between clenched teeth, "That was the best yet," snarled into my ear, already full of blood running from my broken nose. Behavior rewarded will be behavior repeated. I can't count the number of times, the number of different ways I've said that. But with dogs some things are easier: Take a firm stand, be the alpha, the pack leader; then instead of winding up with a broken nose or a few loose teeth, you'll win his undying respect and loyalty. Maybe if I hadn't left school. Derek celebrated with a six pack the night I quit. I stopped bothering to flinch. Didn't even duck. And look what that got me: Held a bottle of Sominex in one fist for three days after he packed some clothes in a grocery bag, called me a cold fish and moved out.

3. Cardinal rule #2: Expect your dog to behave properly

You'll almost always get exactly what you expect of your dog, if you work at it. If you expect it consistently. Ask them: where else in life does that ever work? Don't wait for an answer. The first few weeks are more to retrain the people than their dogs. In six short weeks I try to teach these people how to live with their animals. Actually the animals had also better be learning to live with their people. One or the other will have to be broken.

Or I could say it this way: Expect what you know you'll get, you'll always get what you expect. Is that the same thing?

4. How dogs learn

Just like people, dogs have enough memory to avoid what is unpleasant and repeat only what is pleasant. Tell them to think of the things they've learned without realizing. I never go to double features anymore because of the headaches I used to get, even my old broken nose throbbed. And I've learned to hate certain foods; if I've ever thrown it up, I hate it. (I also got nauseous once while doing yoga. Maybe it was because Derek had hit me in the solar plexus with a law book. I thought the lotus position would calm me down. I've never done any yoga since.) I love to play board games

— complicated ones with lots of rules — but hate two-person-only games and hate to play with people who get silly and play wrong then say, "It's only a game," or "Let's change the rules." Every time Derek missed a question in Trivial Pursuit, he tore the card in half. I never told him, but there were a few other things I didn't care for about him: he was fascinated by the sound of his tires burning rubber; he thought it was funny to make mooing noises at overweight girls; he wouldn't admit to being ticklish; he seemed to live by a law that fast-n-loud is required in everything from music to cars to TV shows to eating. Aren't I better off? I'm always where I expect to be any time during the day. I always know what I'll be doing next. (I never suddenly find myself shoved face-first against a wall, breaking a tooth, one arm twisted behind my back.) The people I see and talk to are always those I expect to see and talk to. And they say the types of things you expect to hear. (Never, "Get your ass back here, we're going to fuck.") I also know what to expect from these classes, so I don't know why I'm bothering to update my lesson plans. There's nothing new to say. I know every class will be the same graceless people tripping over or being dragged around by their wolfish mongrels. Even the application forms are the same; when I ask if the dog is aggressive, I want to know if I'm going to get bitten, but half of them answer as though it's shameful to admit their dog *isn't* aggressive. They'll write, "We're working on it," or "Not enough, that's why I'm taking this class." This one will be no different.

5. *Praise your dog*

Week #2

1. Review Praise

I always have to review this several times. Why am I still thinking about the guy who stayed after class last week to ask how to praise his dog. He has a silky black-and-white mongrel bitch named Tanya. I usually learn the dog names. (But guys like this one seldom have bitches and usually use names like Magnum or Corvette, Dinger, Suds or Max.) He waited patiently while some blowhard told me all the things his hippy-dog (neck kerchief) could do already, like open doors and fill his own water dish. The guy with the bitch was listening and I saw him smile. I'm not sure if he smiled because the blowhard was the kind of guy he'd like to listen to while having a beer in the parking lot at the beach, or if he was laughing because the blowhard was an asshole. I didn't care. I'd seen him smile during class at all my old built-in jokes. One of those flash-of-lightening smiles — electrical current and all — made me almost start to laugh when I looked at him, so I sputtered and choked while explaining leash corrections or how to control barking. Don't even remember what I was talking about, yet I can remember the smile in detail. And his dog sits there looking up at him the whole time — all through class and all the time he waited afterward to talk to me. Finally the blowhard left and the guy, Tanya's guy, said he needed advice about how to talk to his dog. His dog who obviously adores him. He said, "I was a marine sharp-shooting instructor for ten years and I was trained to speak differently to different types of people. There's one way to talk to recruits, another way to speak to an officer, and, I know you won't like this, a different way to speak to a woman." Was he speaking to me in the way he'd learned to speak to a woman? Little Tanya just sat there gazing up at him, waving her tail slightly every time he glanced down at her. I could picture them together out at the shooting range, him squeezing off shots at the human-shaped cut-out, the bitch licking his ear for every fatal hit.

He said, "So I don't really know the best way to talk to my dog. I guess I'm a little inhibited, but I want to make sure I communicate with her the right way. Do I have to talk in a high squeaky voice?"

"Talk to her like you would talk to yourself," I said, which is (I didn't say) like thinking out loud — just be careful. A comment made to myself or the wall, but spoken carelessly in plural pronouns, "We should maybe do the laundry more often. It reeks." Later on the next day — nothing on his face, no hint in his voice — Derek said, "Get outside and do your laundry." All my dirty underwear scattered on the sidewalk and lawn in front of the pavement — and some were quite old with stains in the crotches — I've done the laundry once a week ever since.

Tanya gently stood and put her front feet on the guy's leg. He held her head for a moment and she shut her eyes. I said, "There's nothing wrong with your relationship with her, so you must be doing something right. She'll know when you're being phoney, so don't be. Don't be like a Marine when you talk to her."

He laughed, said thanks and left. Maybe he'll stay after every class to ask something. But then he'll leave for good and never realize I occasionally think about his dusty, sweat-streaked face, nose-to-nose with a fuzzy headed recruit, screaming "You stupid fucking asshole." And the flip-side, in dress uniform and white gloves, holding a woman and drying her tears, saying something that seems uncharacteristic, like, "I'll take care of you." Then the combination: field fatigues, dirt and sweat, oiled rifle; deep, ardent voice — not screaming — saying, "Don't worry about these fucking assholes, I won't let them hurt you."

Week #3

1. One more way to say what I've been saying all along: your dog doesn't care if he's the low man on the pecking order. All he wants is to know for sure. Be consistent in your treatment of him.

They should know this already after last week's demonstration of the alpha roll. Grabbed the biggest, huskiest male mutt, didn't even wait for him to display aggression — had him on his back before he could think, then straddled him, lowered my weight slowly over him, holding the skin on the sides of his face in both fists. We were motionless. Then I looked up. I looked up and our eyes immediately met, Tanya's guy. Maybe it was the position the dog and I were in, I remembered Derek's little motto: you can't fight city hall when you have your legs spread and city hall's on top. Yet even though you know it's wrong, you can't argue because you don't know how it could possibly be wrong. What is that different way Tanya's guy speaks to women? He stroked her back through the whole alpha demonstration. Maybe in ten years of sharpshooting, he never killed anyone, never pointed the gun at anyone — turned it into an artform, lovingly perfected, masculinely precise.

2. Getting the dog to come when called

This can be a big help if your dog is on the verge of getting into a fight. Once the fight starts, though, it's too late, no dog is going to turn tail and come back to his hysterical owner. I should know. In the middle of it, the phone rang — how I managed to answer it I'll never know (one arm must have been free somehow); it was Derek's boss. I don't know if his boss heard him say "Go to hell," the phone was already flying across the room, broke a mirror, lay there beeping and whining until it was all over.

Wouldn't this be a better lesson in class with a real illustration. Two dogs could get into it. The real thing, serious dog business, pull the leashes out of their frantic owners' hands. I always picture a dog fight as a twisting, upright tornado of two dogs and a powerful roar in the air. So it could happen in class, before anyone can move there's a cloud of dust and the blood-quickening sounds of a fight-to-the-death. Because of my insurance, I'll have to stop it, so I have to move in and get a hold of one (or both) by the skin on the backs of their necks. This, I know, is an incredibly stupid thing to try to do. But there's only one thing that can save me now: a soldier. Without a gun, he shields me, throws himself over me. But he's smart enough to realize even he can't stop the fight — all he does is get us out of the middle. One of the dogs would eventually have enough and start to run, the other on his heels, the owners all giving chase. The class doesn't end nor is dismissed, it just disintegrates. So only he and I (and Tanya) are left in the dimly lit parking lot. He touches a wound on my arm, but there's nothing to say, so I still don't hear him speak to a woman.

It would seem a contradiction, though, since I saw him leave class last week in a battered yellow Subaru BRAT, stereo blaring, MARINES bumper sticker on the back. Tanya shared the front seat.

Week #4

It's more than half over. Still feels like it's waiting to start. He hasn't stayed after class to ask a question since that first time. When I say, "That's all for tonight unless you have questions," I see him head for the Subaru with Tanya just before I'm surrounded by the inevitable half-dozen with problems. During the times when I'm explaining something and the whole class gathers around, he wears glasses — not sunglasses. He takes them off during training activities. A Marine in glasses. It seems like I have to keep watching him so I can figure out what's so fascinating about it. Does he look at me that way because it's the way good Marines listen to instructions, or does he maybe want to talk to me differently than the way a Marine talks to an officer? Differently than the way he talks to just anyone. Except maybe Tanya.

What's on for tonight....

1. Rudiments of protection training

Teach your dog to bark at people outside the house. Have a friend walk around while you stay inside with the dog encouraging him to bark, barking with him, exciting him to bark.

Might be interesting if I hint or insinuate that there have been several burglaries in my neighborhood, or that I hear noises in the bushes at night, or there's a peeping tom. His shadow flickers outside my windows. It couldn't be Derek again; Derek doesn't know where I live anymore; I won't even mention Derek. Then I'll say, "In this instance you'd want a dog who knows what to bark at." I don't want anyone encouraging their dogs to attack. They may be friendly pets but with the wrong handling could be turned into dangerous weapons. Then maybe after class Tanya's guy will stay with all the question-askers. As soon as one is satisfied and leaves, the others turn questioningly to each other to see who's next. Tanya's guy always indicates 'you go next' and he continues to wait. Then the problem-digger, problem-chewer, problem-licker has finished trying to convince me their problem is impossible to solve — they don't want answers, they want me to agree nothing can be done — when they're all gone, Tanya's guy is still there and says, "No dogs to protect you?" Dogs aren't always enough. "Maybe I could stay with you tonight and scare him off," he'll say.

I should bring an airline crate to class tonight. Tanya will have to have one so she can ride in the bed of the Subaru when her guy gives me a ride home after my '64 Rambler finally chokes out a death-rattle. Amazing that it lived this long — Derek got it for a couple hundred, took it apart three times, cursing at me because he said I didn't deserve my brand new Toyota. A great day when he finally got the motorcycle he wanted so badly. I gave him the down payment. I only got one ride before he cracked it up, even helmetless he was unscratched, as though his skin — the same color all over — was protection enough, the beauty completely invulnerable, all that construction work and his hands still lovely. But the ruined motorcycle—I couldn't afford to replace it. My fault, he said, he'd had to buy such a cheap one. And I had only one ride. Maybe I'll remember it forever: Taking a turn without slowing down, leaning into it like one body, twenty miles later your heart's kicking you as though you ran the whole way. A ride in a Subaru can't be anything like that. But I wasn't given a choice. I'll let him kneel by the window all night with the rifle, although he never has to aim it at anything. In the morning we'll have to decide whether he should come to stand guard every night until the prowler returns. But maybe once will be enough.

Luckily I can teach this class by rote, just go on with saying the things I've said a thousand times before, hardly hear myself saying them.

Week #5

How far have we come? Looked around the class last week — they are actually improving. Big dogs sitting, waiting for a command; walking relaxed beside their owners on a loose lead; staying when told. But I don't remember teaching any of it — describing technique, giving individual help and advice, explaining canine learning patterns...when was I doing all that? I stand there talking, watching Tanya's guy fondle the inside of her ear with his thumb which makes her lean against him with her head tilted back, her legs relaxed, her belly showing, and I don't know what I've been talking about. Can't even pay attention to myself, I must not be a very good instructor. Derek used to say only assholes were teachers. I prefer to call myself a *trainer*. He thought I should get a job as a cocktail waitress so he and his friends could go out and not have to waste so much money on tips. Locked me out of the house when I was fired. Screamed out the window, "What kind of worthless bitch can't even serve beer!" Said I was a snot, that I thought I was too good, a spoiled-little-rich-girl. So I gave him my Toyota for his birthday. I was left with the Rambler, but he never *gave* it to me. He said I'd gotten too much for Christmas and my birthday when I was younger, so it was his job to straighten me out by not giving me presents. Also called me a spoiled brat every time I suggested I could quit punching the cash register at the K-Mart and go back to school. There's nothing stopping me now from going back. Derek predicted I would. But maybe I'll do something he couldn't predict so easily. Join the Marines. Tanya's guy will talk to me like a recruit, our faces less than an inch apart as he screams about what a stupid-fucking-asshole-with-maggots-for-brains I am. I'll smell his skin— sweat and mud and canvas and gunpowder. My knees may weaken, but I'll stand stiffly at attention, maintaining that half-inch of space between us consistently from head to foot, quivering but not touching anywhere. Then, after the formation has gone trotting double-time down the dusty road, after "chow," I'll come back to the range, alone, and he'll be there to lie beside me, show me how to aim the gun, put his cheek beside mine as I glare down the barrel. That's when he'll talk to me as a woman.

Week #6

1. *Ask Tanya's guy where I could get a gun, could I borrow his?*

I know how to find Derek. That little bar where I was a waitress for two weeks. Follow him home. He won't recognize the yellow Subaru trailing him. Derek steps out of the Toyota. His hair is a little longer, a little blonder. He hasn't shaved since yesterday morning. Tanya's guy is quiet and still beside me in the Subaru, parked across the street from Derek's apartment. Derek puts his six-pack under one arm and unlocks his mailbox. I'm moving now — I know Derek won't pause to read the return addresses. The Subaru door blows open, I somersault out, like I learned...somewhere. Crawl on my belly across the asphalt, crouch behind the Toyota, set myself, brace the rifle over the fender. In my sights, his blue eye— but before firing I shout. I want him to know it's me. I want to see his eyes terrified. Derek screams like a girl and runs into the bushes, thrashing around, the mail like large white snowflakes on the lawn. I'm still shouting. I don't know what I'm shouting, just my voice, harsh and wild. Mid-word, I'm hit from behind, slamming my gut and chest into the car's fender, the gun flies out of my hand, skids over the car's hood and rattles into the gutter while I am wrestled to the street, Tanya's guy smothering me between himself and the pavement, the force of his body all over me, and the force of his voice, talking to me like he would talk to himself, "No, no, no, no...." But I'll have to fight him off so I can run to Derek, to hold him until he's no longer trembling, stroke his hair and mumble so low that the only way he can hear me is through his ear pressed against my chest. Tanya's guy is watching, holding the gun, muzzle to the ground, and our eyes meet. Which one should I love, since both are neither real nor imaginary?

Week #7

Graduation

After I hand him his little certificate and he smiles without really looking at me, not even wearing his glasses, and he starts to walk away with Tanya swishing her fanny — maybe like an unanticipated gunshot, like sniper-fire, I'll call out his name, which I don't even know.

Stabbing

💔

Nancy J. Wallace

I didn't call you because
you've stopped taking your medication
for schizophrenia—
it makes me dopey you said and it does,
but the last time you didn't take your meds
heads would roll you said and they did
so I didn't call you because I was literally
afraid you would cut off my hands and feet
and bury me alive —
the way that landlady did

with her tenants and then,
when it was too late to call,
I dug out my heavy black coat,
pulled on my Timberland boots,
tied a scarf around my head,
and opened the door for a walk —

grass sparkled like slivers of the sea you once told me
looked like the inside of oyster shells,
trees crossed one another
sadly,

the moon pounded like my heart did
the weekend no one could find you,
the river shivered with dread
in the black sheets of its bed,

and some seabird screeched emptily
below your window —

still dark;
still no one answers your phone;
still I keep calling you — still I keep stabbing
at the little
square
buttons.

A Mind of Winter

💔

Yona Zeldis McDonough

I remember meeting Robert. It was at a showing of *Triumph of the Will*. Or rather, I remember meeting him again, because we had been introduced earlier that fall while I was having lunch with Mary at a coffee shop so greasy that its thick smell remained trapped in my hair all day. He appeared at the door, tall, rangy form framed by the rectangle of blue autumn air. Mary motioned him over.

"Come join us," she called. "You'll like Rachel. She's only just started at Columbia, so she hasn't had time to become cynical and jaded like the rest of us." He sat down at our table and I remember trying to engage him in some conversation or other. But he ignored me and talked exclusively to Mary all during lunch. I dripped a large blob of ketchup on my blazer, but they were too engrossed in one another to notice. He seemed very smart, if somewhat sarcastic, and I forgot him with the same ease that I forgot the rancid grease smell when I washed my hair that night.

But then I remembered him, and in the theater's dim, crowded lobby, I found him more interesting. He recognized me instantly, and when he came up to say hello, I noticed how he looked at my body quickly and appraisingly. This annoyed me, but I had to admit that it excited me as well.

"Do you want to try and find a seat together?" he asked.

"I'm with a friend," I said, wishing I weren't.

"So am I. But we could all sit together." Unfortunately, *Triumph of the Will* was popular enough to prevent us from finding four seats in a row, and we gave up trying. He sat in back of me somewhere, and I turned around surreptitiously to look at him as Goebbels sputtered excitedly about the glory of the Reich.

***

I found myself thinking about him so often that when I ran into him at the bank a few days later, I wasn't even surprised. He seemed glad to see me and waited for me to finish my transaction so that we could walk uptown together. We parted in front of Avery Hall, and he indicated the new biology building with an eloquent shrug of his shoulder. "I work in there most of the time. My lab is on the tenth floor."

A few days later, I passed in front of the building I now privately thought of as his. But instead of continuing home, I turned suddenly and made the ascent to the tenth floor. The elevator, despite its sleek silver interior, made a terrible throttled sound as it rose. The hall was wide, white and filled with daylight. The doors to the laboratories had tiny rectangular windows, and after peeking through a number of these, I finally saw him, seated and gesticulating earnestly to another seated man. He ran a hand through his hair as he looked up and then he saw me through the glass.

We walked the length of the corridor together, toward a huge window at its far end. Looking down, it seemed we were much higher than ten stories, and my stomach felt queasy from the fear, but also from something like anticipation.

"Look, I really am kind of busy now, but let's have lunch." He named the place where we had eaten with Mary that time. Although we were meeting the next day, it seemed to me that twenty-four hours was a long time to wait.

***

That night, I couldn't sleep. I got out of bed and decided to paint the bathroom door, which I had been meaning to do for some time anyway. The dark green paint glided on like syrup, the shining wet surface mysterious, some deep forest pool. I was delighted; the tiny bathroom was turning into some tropical paradise. The side of the tub was encased in plywood and I decided to paint that too. When I was finished, it looked beautiful, but I was nowhere nearer to sleeping. And I now needed to shower to remove the oily sting of turpentine, but the steam would have ruined the paint job. I got back into bed and read until seven; then I went to my next door neighbor's apartment to shower.

***

At lunch, Robert and I began to exchange deliberate, vital shards of information, carefully putting down a pattern, a mosaic of intimacy. He grew up in Great Neck. He had a sister who had recently given birth to twins; he was mesmerized by watching her nurse his infant nieces. He had been working on his Ph.D. for over five years. He was terrified that he would never get it.

"What about you?" he asked. "Are you in it just for the M.A. or are you on for the long haul?"

"I don't know," I said truthfully, "I've always just sort of liked being in school."

His beautifully-shaped hands toyed with the salt and pepper shakers on the table.

"What's your speciality?" he wanted to know. "Modern? Baroque?"

"Medieval," I said.

"Medieval? Churches and stained glass—that's what you like?"

"It's the transformations," I said. "Water into wine. Matter into spirit. And the saints, I like the saints: the Virgin, Mary Magdalen."

"Mary Magdalen?" He smirked. "You're kind of weird, you know. But that's all right." He reached under the table and squeezed my hand.

Standing at Avery again, I was keenly aware of the small, interwoven red bricks beneath our feet, their rosy color vivid, glowing. The shrubs surrounding the building were still richly green and the sky, a brilliant blue.

"I'll be talking to you," he said. He turned away, and I watched his retreating form with pure elation.

***

The next time I ran into him was at Shermerhorn Hall, the building where all of the art history classes are held. I was surprised, but Robert explained that the building once housed the natural sciences as well as the arts, and that some of the more advanced graduate students were given offices here. He was on his way up to his; did I want to see it? The door was an old and beautifully grained oak, with a brass knob. A frosted pane of glass comprised its upper half, and I found myself thinking that if I were passing by, his lithe shape would be discernible through its surface.

He unlocked the door and walked in ahead of me, immediately going over to the window, which faced Amsterdam Avenue.

"There's a great view from up here," he said with his back to me. It suddenly occurred to me that he was nervous. A comforting thought, since his self-confidence seemed at times to border on arrogance. I crossed the room to stand next to him and placed a hand very gently on the nape of his neck. My hand moved slowly down the surface of his back, polishing the bones through his flannel shirt. When it reached the base of his spine, he turned, took my face in his hands and kissed me.

***

The next night, we had dinner in a Thai-French restaurant on West 83rd Street. We stayed at his apartment, which turned out to be above a coffee shop as greasy as the one at which we met. In my first delirium, I even liked that rancid smell — it seemed so raw, so sensual.

In the morning, I attempted to make the disheveled bed while he was showering. "Don't bother," he said, as he emerged from the bathroom loosely clad in a towel. He was still wet and water was dripping onto the wood floor. "I never do it."

"It was made last night when we got here," I said.

"That was because I hoped you'd be coming home with me."

I was aware that it was difficult to appear debonair and nonchalant while naked and still wet, but he managed to do it. As I kissed him, my blouse slowly began to soak up the water from his body.

***

"You always smell terrific!" he said several days later as he buried his face in my neck. "What's the name of that perfume you wear?"

"Channel No. 5."

"Are you kidding? No one wears that stuff anymore, except maybe Adele Glassman." I had never heard of Adele Glassman, although I had some vague idea that she might be a famous opera singer. I didn't know whether to admit my ignorance; he could be so disdainful.

"Who is Adele Glassman?" I risked asking.

"Adele Glassman is short, fat, fifty-nine years old and my mother's best friend," he said, yanking off my sweater as my winter-dry hair crackled with electricity.

***

In late December, Robert had bronchitis. We were in his bed, watching reruns on television. During a commercial, he got up, draped the blanket around him like a refugee and went into the other room. I heard the sound his bare feet made on the kitchen linoleum, and the small, sucking sound of the freezer door being pulled open. He swore softly. When he appeared in the doorway again, I asked him what was the matter.

"I was sure there was some ice cream in there. Or maybe sherbet..."

"Your throat feeling bad?"

"Terrible."

"I'll go get some."

"You don't have to, that's okay." But I was already up, zipping my boots. "What flavor?"

Broadway was seedy, bright, lively, the way it was on a week night. No tourists, only the inhabitants, pouring out of the now closing or closed libraries, headed home to rambling high ceilinged apartments or out for beer, pizza, coffee, pastry. It wasn't very cold yet, and I walked slowly down to 110th Street. I bought the sherbet, also several magazines and the next day's newspaper. I let myself back into the apartment with his key. The television was still on, although he was curled up, not watching. His back offered a mute invitation. I sat down, softly traced the spine.

"They didn't have raspberry—how about rainbow?" He was asleep by the time I had finished showering, breathing in hoarse labored breaths. I watched the late movie with the sound turned down very low, savoring the heat from his body. Although he liked my pampering, I could tell that he hated for me to see him when he was sick. As I fell asleep, it occurred to me that although I may have thought vulnerability was the golden link by which love was forged, he probably wouldn't have agreed.

***

Robert was bent over at the waist, pale blue pants — too thin, too light for this time of year — pulled tightly to reveal firm, lean thighs. He was inspecting coffee, carefully sniffing the beans in their burlap sacks, and studying the names as if trying to establish a connection between the exotic images the names evoked and the glossy brown nuggets. During this investigation, his down parka and tee shirt rode up, exposing a bit of back I had come to know well. I put a hand on it possessively, but he shook me off as he stood up. I flushed, hoping that the girl behind the counter hadn't seen.

"A pound of French Roast," he said to her with his most charming smile. She was so pretty, I thought with alarm. He wiped his glasses with a tissue while she made change and smiled back at him; it was dusty down there with the beans. I watched, envious, as he cradled the fragrant package to his chest.

"Did you want something?" he asked, finally looking over his shoulder at me. Then he pushed the door open with his free arm and waited for me to follow.

***

I had always liked his room, the soft, diffused light, the white, soft bed. Although a Spartan about many things, Robert refused to sleep on the unyielding wood covered by a thin layer of foam that was then so popular, preferring instead this low bed with its smooth white sheets, white down comforter and pillows, everything full and enveloping. He was sitting with his legs outstretched, very deliberately not touching me. I sat curled up, arms around my knees, boots discarded on the floor. I was playing with, not drinking, a glass of white wine. This was a hand-blown glass, and I could see two tiny bubbles trapped in the stem. I dipped my fingers in, and rubbed around the rim to wet it. The tiny, squeaky sound filled the awkward silence.

Robert was angry with me. When he had phoned me earlier in the day about our date, he couldn't decide on a time, or a restaurant. Finally he just dispensed with dinner altogether, saying peevishly, "I'm going to be busy with this experiment until late. I'll just grab a bite myself and you can come over to my place around ten."

After that I knew that I could not face my mole-like existence in Avery's subterranean stacks. I could imagine with perfect clarity the enormous volume on Romanesque architecture that I should have been reading, its old, dried pages crumbling noiselessly as I turned them, attaching themselves to my wool skirt; the steady, infuriating hum of the flourescent lights, the attractive but mercilessly uncomfortable new chairs that would not support my back while I read. I decided against Avery that day.

Instead I spent the day in my apartment, drinking tea and eating cookies while I read back issues of fashion magazines. One well-known beauty expert advocated conditioning the hair with warmed oil before shampooing, particularly in the winter months, when hair was apt to be "dull, lifeless and dry." In the kitchen, I located a half bottle of peanut oil. Pouring it into a small pot, I stripped off my nightgown, got the comb and a towel and waited. I was just about to pour the oil over my head, but thought that it would be easier if I combed it through my hair instead. I dipped the comb into the pot and when I pulled it out, I saw that the teeth had sprouted; they were now elongated and curled like the tendrils of a deep sea plant.

When I could safely dip my finger into the oil without wincing, I rubbed it into my scalp vigorously, wrapped my head in a towel and sat down dutifully to wait. My head smelled like a Szechuan kitchen. After the third and even fourth washings, it was still pretty pungent. It took six separate shampoos to get the smell out, by which time any hair conditioning benefits were utterly obliterated.

Finally I had a sip of wine. It tasted awful. Robert began to make a list, resorting in this awkward moment, to a familiar, even scientific mode of expression. He said his work, and he repeated this several times for emphasis, was the single most important thing in his life and no relationship, certainly not the one with me, could be allowed to interfere with it. Which brought him to the second point: I wanted this relationship more than he did, which made it unbalanced, like an unequal equation, and therefore unsound. Further, I displayed my affection too openly, was forever touching him in public and kissing him on street corners. I knew he hated this so why did I persist? Finally, he wanted a woman much more sure of herself, more confident, whose work was really important to her. Which obviously was not the case with me.

I put down the wine glass and shifted position so that the white expanse of bed between us had disappeared. I was facing him and close enough to reach over and touch his face, which I did. He allowed me to remove his glasses. Then I peeled off my sweater and let it fall on the floor. He remained motionless for a minute, then leaned over to unhook my bra. His face moved to my breasts and my arms went around him and just then, it didn't seem to matter that I kissed him in public or wasn't committed enough to my work. Without disengaging from the embrace, I leaned over to turn out the light; I didn't want him to see the tears that had started to fall and that kept falling the instant he touched me.

In the morning, when we were getting ready to leave, I halted his progress across the room and kissed him, my hands caressed by his fine, silky hair.

"Just once, can't you be a little bit late, why do you have to be there so early..." I said into his shirt, knowing, even as I said it, what the answer would be. Although I could feel his erection pressing against my hip, he pulled away and went to the closet to get our coats.

***

Several weeks passed, in which I didn't hear from him. Nor

did I attempt to make direct contact. But I began searching for him. Constantly. Emerging from the library, I scanned the faces that moved past me, anxiously seeking his. I stood in front of university buildings I knew he frequented, tying my scarf against the bitter cold, always looking. I sniffed out the scent of men who resembled him, the same fine hair, perhaps, or walk and I followed the trail, unwilling to relinquish the fantasy that it might, in fact, be him. I gazed into windows of supermarkets, banks, laundromats, craned my neck to peer into the buses that ran down Amsterdam Avenue and up Broadway. After all of that I don't know why I was so surprised when I finally did find him, seated unassumingly in the Cuban-Chinese restaurant that was a block from where I lived. A more haphazard glance and I would have missed him, but obsession had made me keen.

I decided to go in. The restaurant was cheap and good and, as usual, very crowded. Wading past the students and the sprawling Hispanic families, it seemed to take me a long time to reach the table. I could see that Robert was leaning over to say something quietly to the companion seated across from him, who was, thank God, male.

"Well," he said, looking up. "Fancy meeting you here!"

"Why?" I said. "I practically live around the corner. You must have forgotten."

"Oh, no, of course not." At least he had the grace to look uncomfortable. "Murray," he said, directing his attention to the somewhat awkward man who was such a perfect foil to Robert's own sleek good looks. "Murray, I'd like you to meet Rachel; Rachel, this —"

"I think we've met," I said, remembering that far-off autumn night at *Triumph of the Will.*

"Nice to see you again." Murray looked at me pityingly and I had a sudden desire to slap him; why did he think I wanted his pity? I turned to Robert.

"So how's your work going?" I asked.

"Driving me crazy as usual," he said. "How's your work?"

"Not very well. In fact, I'm thinking of dropping out."

"Oh really?" When he said it, I saw for the first time how disdain made his face less handsome, almost ugly.

"Yes, really."

"Don't you think you should stick it out? At least until the end of the year?"

"What for?"

"Nobody likes a quitter," he said, smiling as if he had just paid me a great compliment.

"I guess you're right," I said smiling, too, although I very much wanted to cry. Instead I turned away and kept moving toward the door.

First Marriage Again

💔

Marilyn Elain Carmen

He is sick
can't walk
can't hardly talk
I didn't even recognize
his voice over the telephone

I used to call so much
in those years past and frozen
First the calls
were asking him to come and see me
or telling him that I bought
a brand new pair of men's argyle socks

When he wouldn't come
I'd take a handful of asthma pills
and call back to say goodbye
I wanted him to take me away
from suffering my crazyness
I was afraid sometimes to open
my eyes in the morning
afraid the sun would burn me to death
if I went outside
or that a robin would attack me
in springtime
forcing me in its nest
for her babies to eat

Then my babies came

and I was still calling him
asking when he was coming home from work
or telling him one of the babies was sick
to make sure that he didn't spend up his pay check
But he'd spend it anyway
and then I'd have to keep my wallet
in the oven
so he wouldn't steal the rent money

One day he left home
When I found out where he was I called him
and he told me
that he had been attacked
by a high yellow woman
with string straight hair
who never put her wallet in the oven
Before he said goodbye
he told me not to call back
But I kept on calling
and sometimes he would come

Now one of our babies
is having a baby
and I called again
and I cried for him
for all those years
past and frozen
and the wasted telephone calls

*l*ove *b*etrayed

One Hit to the Body

💔

Mary Shen Barnidge

It has a funny-sounding name,
But there's nothing funny about a dumdum bullet.
Designed to fragment upon impact,
This deadly scatter-round enters by one door
But exits many. For this reason,
It was outlawed by the Geneva Convention of 1929,
For the rules of chivalry demand
A quick and clean kill.

You see, all's *not* fair in war —
But love has no such agreements,
So if you see some small, almost invisible scar
worn by an empty-eyed veteran,
Never assume that their initial wound was slight.
There are no restrictions on issue to lovers of .375 Magnums,
And many a mortal has been hit by a single, superficial shot,
Only to find their heart left hollow as a burnt-out casing.

Blackmail

Susan Hawthorne

bitter
blackmail

your words
are your weapon

tie me down
cut me open
then twist

do not
you must not

riffle through emotions —
turn what was into its opposite

confuse
divide

draw it out
— the confession

throw it back
invert

divide
confuse

yes yes
all right

I am yours

The Crush

💔

Eileen Elliott

The last time I saw Jack was at an A.A. meeting on the Fourth of July, Independence Day, at the West Side Y on 63rd Street.

I had just written him a final farewell the day before. After a few pages of an analysis of his personality, based on Karen Horney's *Neurosis and Human Growth,* I concluded with, "I hope you die an imminent, grizzly, prolonged, and unbearably painful death, and my only other hope with regard to you beyond that, is that I hear about it, so as to enjoy your suffering. I hate you. Janis. P.S. Please don't try to contact me for apologies. My heart is closed."

I didn't mail the letter. Friends said he'd think I'd gone off the deep end.

We had met at an A.A. meeting the previous May. I didn't think Jack was particularly attractive at the time. He was tall, though not exceptionally so, and very thin. His head seemed too large for his body and there was a grayish tinge to his complexion. His hair was cut close at the sides and left longer on top, so that it stood straight up about a quarter of an inch. I caught him watching me, from the corner of my eye, as I walked across the room with the collection basket. He seemed quite interested as his gaze ran down my hips and the back of my legs, but then the faintest cloud of disapproval showed when it landed on my red and black lizard skin cowboy boots.

He talked at the meeting for a long time; mostly about his miserable childhood and about how he alienated people by saying what was on his mind. Though I identified strongly, I thought he was arrogant. When the meeting was over I said to him, "Don't expect people to look upon you kindly for telling the truth." "Quite the contrary," he replied. "They'll crucify you for it," I said. He laughed. We clicked.

I was floundering at the time. I had been sober five years and my life was going nowhere. A.A. said things would get worse before they got better, and they certainly had. I had moved five times in five years because of intolerable living situations. My relationships during this time were brief and disastrous, so were my jobs. I was broke constantly and at odds with the world. My life didn't interest me in the least.

Until I met Jack.

I quickly became intoxicated by him. He was intelligent and perceptive in ways that I was not. He wasn't intimidated by people. He knew how to get what he wanted, and he didn't compromise his standards as far as I could tell.

Jack said that every relationship of any kind was a political situation. Everyone wanted something and it was this wanting that made them vulnerable. He said I had to give myself what I needed, not look for it from other people. He said I had to choose what was best over what was easiest. He told me to listen to the people who tried to help me — therapists, A.A. groups — but to rely on my own perceptions and make my own decisions. Integrity was the important thing. "The pain doesn't matter, that's just life," he said. "You'll always be in pain."

Jack said he'd realized the importance of integrity by having lost all of his. He had been a successful musician, a saxophone player, years ago, but ended up as an alcoholic and junkie with nothing. When I met him he had been clean and dry for four years and was making his living doing studio work.

Part of the reason I think I fell for Jack was that he made me feel cared about in a way no one ever had before. He said he wanted the relationship to last, that there would be things we found out about each other we wouldn't like, but we would work through them. He said we must have both been abducted by the same band of aliens who'd scrambled up our brains in the same way. He brought me over picnic dinners late at night. He walked me home when I didn't stay over, or paid for a taxi. He took me to yoga classes. After one class he picked me up and carried me down the street, kissing me for a whole block. He was beaming. He took me to my first symphony, a Mahler concert at Carnegie Hall. He leaned forward in his seat, gripping my hand and looking back at me and then again at the orchestra during the crescendos, as though he didn't know which was more beautiful or more exciting.

I never felt as happy with anyone as I did those first few weeks with Jack. He split the world wide open for me.

The sex wasn't that great though. Sex with Jack. It was weird. The first couple of times we tried he couldn't get it up. Frankly, it disturbed me, but I figured we just needed time to get comfortable. He said, "I must be more nervous than I thought." He said, "I must be out of shape sexually." That was a new one. "How can you be out of shape sexually?" I asked. "Only a woman would ask a question like that," he told me.

Then the first few times we did have sex he faked orgasms. But I figured, I'm not going to ask him about it. He just needs time. The thing is, I think he really resented me having orgasms because he would bring me right to that point and then he would stop. I couldn't get up the nerve to say anything to him. I didn't want to embarrass him in case he really was sexually inept. Maybe time would solve this problem, too.

I was so excited and relieved to be with Jack, that I didn't care in the beginning that I was exhausted. I commuted a total of four and a half hours a day out to New Jersey. I'd leave his apartment at 6:30 in the morning and return at seven that night. We'd stay up until one. Jack wasn't exhausted because he had taken some time off from work and he was on vacation from school. When I couldn't take it anymore, and finally suggested something like, maybe I could go to sleep at eleven instead of one, we argued. "So I guess we won't see each other during the week anymore," Jack said. And that was that. We didn't.

Everything changed. He began criticizing me constantly. I wasn't assertive enough. He was tired of making the plans. He wanted me to initiate things. Then when I would call and ask to see him, he'd reject me. "What do you want to do, look at me?" He said I wasn't a priority in his life, that his consciousness was twice as expanded as mine, that I was suffering from a condition clinically termed "morbid dependency" and he wasn't equipped to deal with it, that the only need of his I met was sexual; and that he could get caught up in a fantasy just as easily as anyone else. "People try each other out, and if it doesn't work they move on," he explained. "It wasn't my intention to hurt you."

Actually, it worked out quite well for Jack, because the end of our relationship coincided perfectly with the end of his vacation from school, and his return to work.

So.

It had been two weeks since Jack and I had broken up when I ran into him at the meeting on 63rd Street. I got there late and the place was packed. I felt his eyes on me as soon as I walked through the door, but at first glance I didn't see him anywhere. I took the only empty seat, on a stiff green bench near the entrance. About half-way through the meeting I spotted him, wearing a bright purple shirt, sitting in the third row on the far side of the semi-circle. It was like being thrown a curve from left field. My heart started pounding and my mouth went dry. I wanted to run.

The meeting was over and a crowd of people were milling around. I kept my eye on him and remained in my seat. He had to walk by me to get to the door. He started walking in my direction, but stopped to chat with someone.

"Hey, what are you doing today?" an actor friend of mine, Harry, asked while giving me a hug. He was wearing a t-shirt, shorts and a baseball cap, and he was carrying a mitt in his hand. "A bunch of us are playing softball over in the park. You want to come?"

"Thanks," I said, "but I don't really feel like it. Besides, I'm not dressed for it." I was wearing a white blouse, slacks and sandals.

"I know, you'd rather sit home and isolate, right?" Harry asked.

"Maybe."

"Okay, have fun. If you change your mind you know where we'll be."

Those A.A. people drove me crazy. They always thought they knew what was best for me.

I didn't want it to look like I was hanging around, so I walked outside into the sunlight. A few people were sitting on the stoop, smoking cigarettes and talking. Jack wasn't out there.

Looking toward the park, I thought of the last weekend we'd spent together. How he's pinned me against a stone wall in Riverside Park, crushing me with his body as he kissed me with the sky all orange and pink as the sun went down over the water.

I turned around and walked back into the lobby. Jack was walking out. He saw me and immediately looked down at his feet.

"Jack," I said with a twinge of sudden alarm.

"Hey, how ya doing?" He was smiling. "What are you doing today? Let's go for a walk."

We went outside and made a right, walking past Houlihan's.

The smell of charcoal broiled steak blasted out with the hot air from the grills in the kitchen.

"Aggh, this is disgusting," Jack said. "I swear sometimes I walk by here and you can actually see big black billows of dead cow smoke."

"I think it smells good."

He looked at me and shook his head. "You carnivores are all the same."

"So what's new? How've you been?" My lips stuck together as I spoke. I was sure there was a fine line of dried white saliva where they met.

"I'm okay," he said. "Same old stuff — working, practicing, going to school. How are you? How's the job?"

"I'm fine. Work's okay. They're making a lot of cutbacks though. I'm the only one in the department who hasn't been cut back to three days a week."

"Why are they making cutbacks?" Jack asked.

"Because they're losing money."

"What AT&T losing money! I guess everyone made the right choice. They picked MCI," he drawled. "So how is it living with your brother?"

"Pretty good," I took a deep breath and exhaled as I spoke. "We get along really well. Albert's quiet and he works at night, so we don't see too much of each other. He also has an eye for interior decorating, so he's fixed the place up."

"Naturally, he's gay right? It goes with the territory. Hey that's one good thing about having a gay brother, at least you don't have to worry about incest."

"It's a plus," I said.

Jack started walking north on Broadway, in the direction of his apartment building. He turned around surprised I wasn't following, came back to where I stood and stared into my eyes. His looked like they had tiny lights behind them. Before when we were together and his eyes shone like that I thought, *he's crazy about me.* But standing there on the corner I realized it wasn't me at all. He folded his arms over his chest, impassive, invincible. "So what's on your mind?" he asked.

My pain was a palpable thing now, aching in all of my hollows like some cruel amoeba. I knew there was rage somewhere inside of me, but there was something else, too; something darker and more powerful. My self-esteem had disintegrated in the few minutes I'd spent talking with Jack.

The feeling was like in a dream I'd had as a child, that something in my room was crushing me. I was in bed and the thing had me crumpled up into a tiny ball at the bottom, grinding my chest into my knees and my head against my knees and my feet into my buttocks. It kept crushing and crushing, even though I was already crunched up as small as I could be. It wasn't enough. I thought my bones would break. Finally the pain became so intense I woke up, and there I was — all contorted into a crushed little ball beneath the covers at the bottom of my bed.

Staring at Jack I knew. The crushing thing was *inside* of me. His temples seemed grayer, and there was a weariness about him. He doesn't give a shit about me, I thought, looking away.

"Nothing," I answered. "Nothing's on my mind. Did you like the meeting?"

"I rarely *like* a meeting," Jack said. "Those people are too full of themselves for my taste. Did you hear that guy who said he wants to buy an American flag so he can burn it while it's still legal. I'd like to burn his ass, the motherfucker." He paused. "Did you like the meeting?"

"It was alright," I answered. "I think meetings are good." I didn't know what to say.

"What do you mean, *good?*"

"I mean I think they help people live normal lives."

"Normal?" He was incredulous. "What's normal? There's no normal. Normal is alcoholism, drug abuse, murder, rape. Did you hear they finally found Kennedy guilty of Chappaquidick? Normal is a reputable guy takes you home from a party and you wind up dead at the bottom of a river. That's normal, and you're not going to get anywhere as long as you keep walking around with some kind of fantasy about what normal is."

As he spoke, he watched the women walk up and down the street, his eyes moving over their bodies like he was grading U.S. Choice beef. I inadvertently made a preening gesture by tucking in my blouse in the back with both hands. Jack stared at my breasts a minute then looked away.

I thought of all the energy I had wasted on people who didn't care about me, on Jack. How I had excused or distorted their cruelty or indifference, never considering the possibility that they really didn't care.

"Well, I gotta get something to eat," Jack said, jerking his head in the direction of his apartment building. "So, ah, I guess I'll see you around." He was still smiling.

"Bye," I walked away abruptly.

"Hey, take care of yourself," he called after me. "And be careful, you know, everybody doesn't always have your best interests at heart."

"Thanks," I said.

Scumbag! Where was my self-esteem? How had I lost it so completely? It had been sucked out from under me imperceptibly, and I could only recognize it reflected back through Jack's touch or reassurance. No. It hadn't been sucked out from under me. I had *given* it to Jack for the asking, for the promise of love.

Walking home by way of the park, I tried to come to some sense of who Jack was, but I couldn't; who was I for that matter, if I could be deceived so completely? I felt like the world was shifting and I was lost again.

Then I saw Harry and some other familiar faces spread out in one of the diamonds, so I sat on a bench to watch the game. I didn't know the names of most of the people playing, but I recognized their faces from the meetings. They said things like: I didn't drink today; I didn't get high today. They held onto their lives one day at a time even when they didn't really feel like it.

Harry saw me and waved. I waved back and sat on a bench to watch the game. I watched into the night until the last player slid home, and the lights went out on the playing field.

Honeymoon

💔

Rusane Morrison

Highway out of Vegas,
a rushing gutter of August heat —
cars and signposts hurl past
the slice of my face in the mirror,
my fists round the wheel.

Any conversation
has blown out the windows,
died with your air conditioner
and my luck —
a pair is always
a risky bet.

You've slumped against the door
toward sleep,
your jaw drops
open, waiting.
But the hot air is a brick
thrown down your throat
that wakes you gagging.
Your eyes everywhere,
at me,
like I'm water
you've choked on.

You want the wheel back,
I take the first turnoff.
Dirt road crackles and spits
us toward this reservation store.
"Cooler Inside"

and the aluminum outhouses
glare in the buzzing, thrumming heat.
We get out of your car.

Cigarettes, dust
clotted racks of beads,
a dozen lighters
under duct-taped glass,
their rowed patterns, veined
wasted blue.
I find the spattering air-cooler
and close my eyes.

You ask the young Moapa woman
about fireworks —
sparklers, missles, snakes,
fancy magic
packaged, easy.
"Yes legal
while you're here,"
she says,
"and cheap."

You pull your lip.
"No, thanks,
don't need no
more trouble:
picking up
something,
find out
I can't use.
Wouldn't want
to make that same
mistake
twice."

Kitchen Meditation

💔

CarolAnn Russell

I bought a black hat and fan and
red shoes in Chinatown
while you were thrashing about in
the waves off Alcatraz.
Intricate crocheting,
a wrong moon,
your mother sad
and nothing you could do.

The black man who held my hand
in the operating room
and wiped my tears when the needle pierced
the scar like a paper lantern
would not let the surgeon cover my face.
I am not dead, I joked
and then cried at how close I'd come.
The time you smashed me against the wall
I saw no colors at all,
I heard no serious music.

The kitchen has a window like an eye
that opens to a maple tree.
The wind comes and goes.
When the wind comes and goes
I watch green leaves describe the movements
in the air, in shadow on the table,

I listen to water drops in the sink,
their splunking like a metronome.
What if, they say. What if. What if.

Dusk. I sit in the kitchen, my hands
flat against the table's cold cheek.
It is a violent act — remembering,
piecing what has been torn
into the skeletal whole.
On the sill outside a small bird quivers,
working its tiny chest.

Looking for a Home

💔

Ceil Malek

The first time my husband choked me I was standing in front of the kitchen sink. We'd had an argument about whether his brother could visit our house that weekend. Dave said yes and I said no because I needed to meet a deadline for the publication I was editing. No wasn't what Dave wanted to hear.

He stopped choking before I was unconscious, but not before I was terrified. I called the police and the officer who came to our house wanted to know if Dave had a gun, a knife or if he'd been drinking. The answer to all those questions was no. The policeman looked at my neck and was unimpressed but told me I could press charges. I didn't press them because I didn't want to cause any more problems, but I did decide to leave. I packed a suitcase for my 18-month-old daughter and me, and walked out the door.

In a state of confusion, I knew I needed to find a place where I could be alone to sort out what had happened. After driving aimlessly for a while, I stopped at a bed and breakfast place, but couldn't get out of the car. I drove on, stopping at several motels, but still couldn't get out of the car. Finally I had driven so long and was so tired and hungry that I knew I had to choose a place to stop soon. I found a place with cottages for rent, paid for one night's stay with my credit card and unpacked.

I felt very disoriented. I remember how bleak the place was with insects crawling on the floor and strange smells that made me wish I were in my own home. I remember crying some but mostly feeling afraid. There was rage lurking below my terror, but I muted it because I knew I had to think about my survival and my daughter's. At the time this pattern of sealing off my anger in a separate compartment left me free to cope with a very threatening situation.

After a restless night, I called my therapist who agreed to see me. I hoped when I told her that Dave had choked me that her reaction would make sense to me. I hoped, too, I could adopt her reaction as my own because I didn't know how I felt. The compartmentalization which seemed to keep me mobilized also left me confused because I wasn't allowing myself to experience my own feelings.

After I told my therapist my story, she said, "What did you do to provoke him?"

I felt accused. Her reaction reinforced my fear that I must have done something very terrible to have caused my husband to choke me. I took responsibility for his abuse and hid the incident as the kind of unspeakable thing I must not mention.

After the unsettling therapy appointment, I called my friend Susan who invited me to stay at her house. I remained the night and then crept out in the morning before she woke up. I wanted to go home more than anything else in the world, so the strangeness and the confusion I was feeling would end. In familiar surroundings maybe I could get some perspective on what was happening to me. I arrived in time for Dave's brother's visit. That was good, I thought. After all, I didn't want to make my husband any madder or alienate his family. I still planned to make my marriage work.

When my brother-in-law departed, I told Dave that if he ever touched me again, I would leave. I think he believed me. I certainly believed what I was saying. I tried to settle in and convince myself that everything was going to be all right. However, in order to do that, I didn't bring my feelings about the choking into the light of day and examine them. Whenever I got close to them, I felt too uncomfortable, so I focused on the life I lived every day — taking care of my daughter, meeting deadlines for my publication, seeing my friends and working in therapy, hoping to make myself into a more acceptable wife.

The fact that I was 35 years old and had a master's degree didn't seem to help me. Neither did the fact that I considered myself fairly liberated and sophisticated. I was trying to make that marriage work as if my life depended upon it. And I suppose I believed that it did. On some level, I thought if I were on my own again, it would be like staying in the cottage where I had spent the night — I would feel completely abandoned, poor and faced with things like crawling insects and nauseating smells.

It was another year before Dave choked me again. I told him

once more that if it ever happened again, I would leave, but even I didn't believe my words this time. I didn't call the police. I knew I didn't have the courage to leave my marriage.

Fortunately during the five years after that, Dave didn't choke me again. Rather than hurting me physically, he was verbally abusive. Our marriage was very tense. We had gut-wrenching fights full of yelling, my tears and slammed doors. I tried to communicate the depth of my feelings to my husband, but I was not blameless in these fights. The times my rage did break through, I tried to retaliate against the man who caused me so much pain. Our marriage was an emotional see-saw. We took turns assuming the roles of victim and perpetrator and the perpetrator always justified the abuse because he or she felt like the righteous victim.

Guilt, confusion and rage left me feeling impotent and even more trapped. I had a second child and when he was about three, I hit my lowest point. Afraid I was dying, I made the rounds of medical doctors convinced that I had cancer of some sort. I saw an oncologist who told me I didn't have lymph cancer, I saw a dermatologist who told me I didn't have skin cancer, and I saw a gynecologist who told me I didn't have cancer of the uterus. I finally realized that my problems were psychological rather than physical and that I needed help badly.

I found a new therapist and although I was unable to really discuss my marriage because I felt so guilty and unsure of myself, I started to work on my own problems. I began to understand how my family of origin, in which harsh words were never spoken and in which there had not been any physical abuse, was abusive anyway. It was there that I first learned to split away from my feelings of rage, fear, sadness, and even happiness. In therapy, I started to feel the feelings I had hidden away since childhood when I had not been heard or seen or responded to.

Therapy made me healthier, but I still wasn't strong enough to leave my marriage. I really wanted my husband to enter counseling. I wanted him to apologize for hurting me and I wanted him to come to see me for the person I knew I was. He finally did consent to therapy, but after one session decided to ask for a divorce. My relief was enormous, but at a deeper level, my terror loomed, that old terror that I would be abandoned if I weren't good enough.

Now it's been a year and a half after our separation and six weeks since our divorce. I'm beginning to realize the abandonment that I'd feared so long did actually happen when I was a child and that I've survived it. With three years of good therapy under my belt, I begin to build the kind of life I'd hoped for. I've realized my goal to teach writing at the university level and I'm working toward other goals I wasn't sure I could ever reach. Most important, I'm beginning to befriend myself. Recently I've been able to experience my own anger without being afraid that I will, like Rumpelstiltskin, stamp my feet until the earth opens below and swallows me. I'm starting to trust the feeling that my rage is good, that it gives me information I need to protect myself. I begin to understand how to defend myself rather than siding with the tyrants (both internal and external) against myself. I start to like myself. And very tentatively, I start to reach out. Of course, I'm wary. I know I made a bad choice when I chose my husband and that I compounded that bad choice thousands of times over by accepting his abuse and by splitting away the rage that would have given me the momentum to act appropriately on my own behalf.

After trying to get home for so many years, I believe I'm finally on the doorstep.

Again

Barbara Ittner

I hated that hand
with its stiff, red fingers,
and bitten down fingernails,
your hand
that slapped my face.
And those full blown lips
that would tighten around a cigarette
or press hungrily against a lover
in dark corners of night,
the lips that said
"I had to do it."

"You were hysterical," you explained,
the word pronounced carefully,
a snake placing venom in dumb flesh.
The lips came together
over clenched teeth,
your mouth now motionless,
eyes alive.

Moments before
I was screaming,
a raw face reflected in the mirror,
heaving something horrible
out of me.
A treacherous spine scraped my throat,
blue-black skin glistened
with my own insides,

long strands of pain
loosening.

One slap broke open the sky,
and just as it was about to leave,
darkness tumbled back inside.
With feet planted firmly in my bowels,
fingers wrapped around my heart,
home again, I felt the demon smile,
I hated you then —
that hand, that mouth, those eyes.
For a moment I hated you,
and then
I hated me.

Married Love

💔

Marilyn Zuckerman

(for Carol DiMalti Stuart)

When he stares intently at your breasts
he is looking for a place to grind in the burning end of a cigarette.

When he investigates your tongue with his
he wants to see how it fits into your jaw; how to tear it out.

When he touches your throat with his lips
he is feeling for a way to slice into the carotid artery.

When his fingers slide over your skull
he is marking the spot where the bullet will enter.

When he enters you he closes his eyes, pretends it's rape.
                               He thrusts deeper and harder.
The knife is only sheathed.

When his hands feel for your buttocks and he separates them,
he peers inside,
imagines plunging his swollen penis in until he makes
the darkness bleed.

Don't open your mail, lift the hood of your car or walk alone
                         He follows you night and day.
                         He can't get enough of your body.
                         He thinks it smells like money.

Going to the Store

💔

Ann Bronson

I'm going to the store now, just going to the store. To get cigarettes. Cigarettes and beer. That's all. There wasn't anything else, was there? I'd better not forget anything, wouldn't want to walk back. Only have one chance to use the car and that's because of the game on TV. The big one, the Bears and that other team. Can't really watch TV with him. Makes me nervous. My stupid fault if the receiver fumbles, my ugly face made the kicker blow the punt. Why am I watching, anyway? Make myself useful and go get some cigarettes and beer.

Here's Adolph's Liquors. Turn in here with my twenty-dollar bill. That's a fifth of whiskey with the twelve pack, that's right, I almost forgot. And the cigarettes. Should I get two packs? I can't decide. What if he runs out before tomorrow morning? If he wakes up at two or three and jabs at the back of my shoulder — jab, jab. His finger a blade from the jacknife of his hand, the tool.

Where's my cigarettes, when the crumpled pack is lying on the floor next to the bed, next to his lighter, next to the overflowing ashtray, next to the beer can, crumpled over, holding its stomach.

Find me a butt, he says, pushing my shoulder hard toward the edge. Pushing my shoulder to get me going, find him a long butt. I know about this, though; I keep a long butt in the drawer in the kitchen, just as I keep a beer in the basement, a can to appease in case I should be blamed, I have fucked up *again*. I get two packs.

Why can't I take care of his wants? Doesn't he pay the bills, go to work every day? Of course, I do, too, but make half as much. Then there's the housework and the kids. But I'm lucky, he says. Who else would have me?

Twenty dollars about does it. I better keep the receipt. He

thinks I save money, hold out on him. He dumps my purse out on the floor, uses his jacknife hand to look for change, leaves the mess on the floor. He walks on my stuff — why don't I clean out this shit? Women carry so much garbage around with them.

Back in the car. Be careful, now. I'm only supposed to be gone fifteen minutes, no fooling around, no calling my mother again. If she calls back, I'm in trouble. She makes trouble; I'm in trouble. The kids make trouble, I'm in trouble. The world makes trouble, I'm in trouble. These are my lessons. I must learn them.

I look in the rearview mirror. My headscarf makes me look dumpy, like an old frowse, he says. But somehow it protects my head. My head hurts from little bumps, bumps from a finger flick. A reminder, he says. Who would think a finger flick could hurt like that? I don't show it, though. Besides, he says it doesn't hurt; it's my guilty conscience that pains me. So I smile instead and he smiles back, two conspirators.

He tries to look into my eyes, hold me still through my eyes. I would drop my gaze to the floor, but then I'm hiding something, something he should be able to see and know about me. What might I be hiding now? He gets agitated wondering what I'm hiding. Edgy, he wants to know, makes me look into his eyes, his eyes that penetrate my head, burn me, send a hot shot of fear through me. What does he think he sees? I close down a curtain behind my eyes. I try to make them innocent, trusting eyes that hurt me to make them. And I don't cry either. That's guilt for my worthlessness, my lack of appreciation, my dumbness.

I see in the mirror that I should cut my bangs. My skin looks white and bloodless. The blood is in the bruise under the bangs, has run out of the other places, the tiny scars around my mouth and eyes.

Better be careful. I can't call in sick again. The shame and disgust is only for home. At work, I have had the flu, fallen down the stairs, walked into a door, tripped over my own stupid clodhoppers. There, I laugh at my own clumsiness, wave my hand and wave the trouble away, rushing off to hide at my seat. I don't wait to hear my laughter fall and dissolve in the pool of silence behind me.

A car door slams next to me. Startled, I realize I've been looking at the mirror and seeing nothing for several minutes. I'll be late! I back the car out and turn quickly and carelessly into the traffic. I'll be late! My heart starts to pound, my head gets hot, my hands cold. I drive too fast, careen around corners, thinking up excuses, reasons, alibis, all in a panic.

I'm sweating now, forcing my foot up from the accelerator to go slowly and casually the last block to the house. I pull in next to the curb, turning the key in the ignition before the car stops rolling. I'm being as quiet as I can, though my heart is as loud as a bass drum being beaten. I grab the bag from the front seat, close the car door with a tiny click. My pace to the house is careful and infinitely slow, but the enormous front door looms in front of me too quickly. I stop, hesitating only for an instant. He is seeing me there, right through the wall. So I go in.

I'm right. He did see me through the wall. He is standing next to the door, looking normal in a sweater and jeans, smiling into my face. He says, "You're late," and takes the bag from my arms. He stands there. I feel confused, fuzzy headed. What now?

I turn to hang up my coat. Then I feel his foot on my butt. He pushes me hard. I stumble forward and fall to my hands and knees. I stay still, afraid I might cry. Then the hot tears do come to my eyes. He stands next to me, bends down and yells into my ear, "I SAID, YOU'RE LATE!!"

I can't move. I'm frozen. I'm staring at a small stain on the rug under my face, a tiny blot there, a tear I lost from my eye by accident, not my fault.

He walks past me to the kitchen, puts the beer in the fridge and comes back toward me. I hear the can hissing as he wrenches the tab. He is ignoring me there on the floor, brushing by, the touch of denim skins my arm like fire. I let my body sink sideways and lie on the rug. The sound of the TV reaches my clouded mind. The score is twenty-one to nothing.

Suspicion

Phillis Gershator

A dull ache
filled my body
and I couldn't tell
if it was you
sleeping with someone else
or my back
breaking in the night

The ache went in and out
out and in
in time to your breath
and the curve
of my splitting spine

Even if I was asleep
the dreampains were real
more real than breakfast
and you
strangely tired in the morning.

Spilled Milk

💔

Pamela Pratt

She was going to play pool after work, she said: Did I want anything when she came back?

A quart of milk, I said, for our coffee in the morning.

Don't we have some?

You spilled it, I reminded her.

When she was late getting back I knew she'd met up with the sweet young thing we'd met in the bar the week before. I need more friends, she'd said to me while buying the baby a drink.

What can you possibly have in common with that dykette? I said.

Maybe I don't rely on talk to get along, she answered back.

At times I know my lover better than she knows herself: this night I knew she didn't have a clue what she was doing. I knew how it would go, every line, every linger of it, and I crawled into bed with my stuffed rabbit Molly, waiting for it all to be over. When she finally came home, she called me from the bottom of the stairs and when I said I was asleep, she crawled into our bed anyway, and cried on my shoulder and confessed. Even though I knew, still I had kept myself from knowing that one part of it: that it had been *she* who *started* it, she who tarried and cajoled, she who took the final responsibility and said — oh, she won't mind.

She needed to be held and so I held her without speaking and consoled her for my loss — our loss. I desired her greatly. Her sex smell scented the air and I felt lust everywhere in her touch, even though I knew it had just recently been satiated. She wanted everything from me, she wanted the words, she wanted me to say that I forgave her — more than that, she wanted to hear that it meant nothing to me, *nothing* — just as it had meant nothing to her.

She wanted me to understand that it was her pain more than mine, the living with this thing she can't control, this impulse that sends her out some nights, a haunted lover. I *had* to tell you, she said. When I didn't bring home the milk you would have known anyway. You always know.

Oh, how I held her and rocked her till her eyes closed in fatigue, though she tried to stay awake until my words came, the comfort that would let her sleep. Oh, how I held her tightly, how I lied.

What We're Thinking
When Rapture Doesn't Happen

💔

Laurel Speer

He felt her fingernails clawing at his back and made a sound of delight although he would have vastly preferred some other method of her signalling her mounting pleasure. Still, he continued to ride her in the manner she seemed to prefer— roughly—and tried his best not to breathe in the heavy perfume she wore or the vaguely oleaginous odour that emanated from her hair.

—Elizabeth George, *Payment in Blood*

It's been 22 minutes by the clock
over his shoulder. I wish he'd hurry
so I can get up and do the laundry...
How could he imagine this pleases me?
...The baby just hit the floor heading
for our bed. Can I finish him?...
This one has ferocious body odor.
How could I have missed that before
he took off his clothes?...
If he doesn't quit with the ritual
nipple twist, I'm going home...
If I say no, he'll punish me in one
of 600 well-documented ploys...
This one goes by a manual he read
in 7th grade...
This one never figured out there are
physiological differences...

This position isn't good...
This one hates women so much, he's trying
to kill me...
It must be my fault.

Evening...

Nina Silver

Evening ...
preparation for rituals loving.
My hair is brushed
the bed soft
and my eyes hard.
You wake from a dream
to another,
beckoning.
You wait in silence
and I look at you without speaking,
avoiding the scars
on the bedclothes.
The wind outside
clips the trees
worrying.
I listen.
Then, hesitating
I slide in
let you keep the pillow
and flatten myself against the wall.

Supervision

💔

Karen Leslie

Once I tumbled down an embankment into a stream. The current was picking up speed and I could hear a cataract crashing around the bend. I fell right into it. I had no choice. It crossed the only road to where I was going.

I had been offered a job at a community mental health agency in spite of the fact that I had no training or experience. The people who hired me, one of whom died of alcoholism within a couple of years, liked the fact that I had been a community organizer. Besides, they weren't working real hard to find people with a lot of experience. It would have been too threatening. Twenty-seven staff members had just quit in protest. The new staff never found out why. We just moved right into Love Canal.

After I got the job, excitement gave way to fear that I was in over my head, and I was losing the only support I had, my therapist, Paula. I had gone into therapy the year before after admitting to myself that I couldn't stop falling in love with women. Paula mostly minimized the intensity of my attachments to women, pointing out that I didn't have any while I was in treatment with her, and she kept trying to tell me I was getting better. She seemed to have a need to impress her supervisor with what a good job she was doing with me. But therapy only served a temporary restraining order on other women. Paula had become the obsession. Inside I knew something was wrong and my dreams kept trying to break up our consensual denial. In one dream I said to Paula, "This is a hell of an intake, but when is the therapy going to start?" I even told her the dream and we both had a good laugh over it. Or maybe she did. As conflicted as the treatment had been, Paula was all I had.

Then right after the start of my new job, Paula began to talk about termination. She'd say things like, "Well the Center doesn't like people to stay in therapy beyond a year." Of course, it all turned out to be about her getting accepted into graduate school and wanting to clear out her caseload.

So there I was, with termination as chronic background noise, getting ready to start "picking up cases" and do therapy, something I understood only through the poor example of my own. I knew I'd have to rely heavily on clinical supervision, but that brought up another problem. I didn't like my supervisor. She was loud, domineering, and arrogant. Besides, I didn't think she knew enough to guide me, and I had the presence of mind to realize that my experience needed to be shaped by a real clinician.

I put in a request for a change and it came through. At first I was quite pleased with Marjory, my new supervisor. She had the right credentials from an excellent school. She was poised and I equated that with professionalism. She spoke rarely at meetings, but did so with authority. I didn't take much notice when she suddenly put aside her faded slacks and began showing up to work in silk blouses and long skirts. But it wasn't too long after that I went into hyper-alert.

At the end of our first hour of clinical supervision, she stopped me as I was going out the door and said, "I want to get to know you better. Not just as your supervisor. I mean socially." Then she invited me to join her and some other staff on a camping trip. She quickly added that other supervisors and their supervisees were going. I was stunned by the abrupt change in directions. I needed her for training, not friendship. A boundary had been crossed, and I knew it.

Even though I didn't like the feel of it, a part of me was intrigued. I was vulnerable. After all I was in treatment because I couldn't stop falling in love with women. I couldn't hide it; the cataract was looming. I told Paula right away. I said, "She's trying to seduce me." Paula didn't like my bringing this up. It was spoiling the termination and threatening her ability to stamp "Much Improved" on my file. She jumped in to dam the water. "No," she said, "that couldn't be true. She has her Master's degree in social work." That stumped me. What I needed was someone to help me resist Marjory's invitation. No one did.

The camping trip set the pattern in my relationship with my "supervisor." Marjory would move in close with the bait and then jerk it up like I was some kind of brook trout. It was a strategy that left me simultaneously panting with lust and writhing with guilt. On the first night, she suggested a midnight walk and quickly got me talking about my alcoholic mother, another subject Paula hadn't been much help with. Marjory made a few insightful pronouncements, which I took to be the comforting words of a deity, "a real therapist," and I was on the verge of feeling profoundly cared about when she brought her face in close to mine and said it was time for bed. She quickly turned away from me and walked back to the cabin, merged with the others, acted as if she had never laid eyes on me and set up her gear as far away from mine as possible. That was her approach, to reduce me to the essence of vulnerability, leaving me with about as much ego strength as the center of a crushed green grape, and then, in the words of Bob Dylan, "act like we never have met." You couldn't have pulled me apart from her with the Jaws of Life.

Within a few weeks, the "MSW" would drive me to my therapy appointment as she spoke of how attracted she was to me and, moments before the session was to begin, thrust her thick tongue into my mouth. I would stumble into Paula's office, my faced flushed, confused, sexually aroused, not knowing I had just been raped, and announce, "We just kissed outside your office." I was desperate for Paula's help in releasing me from Marjory's control. Instead she blanched and changed the subject. "I thought we'd talk today about how you're feeling about termination." And when she told me I was "ready to terminate," I would say, "I think I'm in a crisis. I don't know how to get out of this relationship. She's my supervisor. I can't just go and ask for another. I'm new and they already made one change for me." And the response would come, totally dismissing the problem I was raising. "Don't worry. You'll get out of it." Paula's false ego, needing to see me as a successful "piece of work," fed my own. If my therapist thought getting out would be that easy, so could I. I had no knowledge of how many rocks I'd have to bash my head against, before I would get out of that stream.

Given how vulnerable I really was, as well as the lack of support from my therapist, it's incredible how much time I managed to carve out for myself to think it over. I really wanted some space to explore my homosexuality and I actually asked my husband's permission to have it. He refused. I had two small children that I was ignoring in the process and the whole relationship with Marjory felt incredibly wrong. In order to create time to be with her, I had to lie to my husband and claim we needed to get together after work to discuss cases. We actually did talk shop in these off-hours, but it was only because our own case was impenetrable.

One night Marjory called me up, after having been particularly distant and silently hateful for a couple of days, and read me a poem she wrote to me. It was the most erotic thing I ever heard. I can only remember one line, after her finger had slowly descended down my body, how she wanted to "write her name on my belly." She never would show me the poem, probably because she didn't want any incriminating evidence lying around. Soon after, I told her I was ready for sex.

We agreed to meet at her apartment on a Sunday morning. I didn't have much time and she knew it. When I got there, she said, "Let's go for a run." I followed. We ran, we sweated, we returned. She asked me how I was feeling. I didn't know what to label what I was feeling and I didn't want to incur her displeasure, so I said, "Turned on." If she asked me today, I'd know better. "Terror," I'd say. She said, "I'm not aroused, but let's give it a try." For the next hour she stared at my vagina while I pretended to enjoy it. That was the sex. Someone inside of me with a small voice was peeping, "Is this all there is?" I went home to a husband who was furiously insulating the attic in a quiet rage over something he just couldn't seem to put his finger on. I called Marjory that night. She was the only one I could think of to call for relief from the pain she was causing. She said, "I went to the movies after you left. It was great. I had sexual fantasies about you all day." I told myself that meant everything was alright.

I felt compelled to try to make the sex work. A part of me cared for her and believed she truly cared about me, but then she'd parade around work without giving me so much as a nod. One day I was upset when a male staff member, an ex-convict, threatened me, so I did what I was supposed to and went to my supervisor. She blamed me for provoking this man. In yet another supervisory session Marjory said, "You can't give me enough of your time. I need a more fulfilling relationship. This has to stop." I cried. I felt mildly relieved, and said okay, taking her at her word. She came up behind me as I walked out to my car, touched my head and said, "I just love the smell of your hair."

Then I reached the waterfall. Paula had gone on to graduate school, in such denial of my crisis that she didn't even suggest another therapist. I found out that Marjory really didn't have time for me, since she was pursuing a man who was the Executive Director of the entire agency, as well as the lesbian partner of another social worker. Homicide started to look like a pretty reasonable response. Instead, I decided to report her to the woman who was in charge of the section of the agency where we worked, Beth. I assumed the worst, that I would be fired along with Marjory, but my rage needed an outlet. I wanted justice.

I knew this thing was going to blow wide open and if my husband was going to find out, I wanted it to happen through me. When I told him, he said, "That's the most disgusting thing I ever heard." He left and didn't come home until late that day. He had decided to forgive me. Within a week he had called Beth and threatened to report Marjory to the Board of Ethics for Social Workers. Whatever the director told him, it caught him off guard and he went back to blaming me.

Before he made his call to Beth, I had my own meeting with her. I thought it would be simple — I would describe the seduction and we'd both be terminated. Three things came out of that meeting, each more bone-crushing than the next. First she leered and said, "Well, I'm Marjory's supervisor so she was only acting out my feelings toward you." Then, when I protested, she told me in a mean way, "You need therapy." That's all I needed to hear since I was barely defending myself against Paula's abandonment. The last result of our meeting came shortly afterwards: I got the word that Marjory had been promoted to a job I had applied for first.

I was so devastated by this time that I didn't have the where-withal to quit for many months. A part of me felt I should stay to show Marjory up, to prove that she hadn't destroyed me. When I reached out for help to some of our mutual friends, I was politely distanced. It seemed they either wanted to maintain friendships with both of us or openly judged me for being adulterous. I felt very isolated and I was in a constant rage over witnessing her flirtations. Once I thought I saw her driving somewhere and I chased her in my car, with a murderous, insane feeling. My dreams provided the only outlet. In one I repeatedly slapped her across the face saying, "I hate you." In another I told her a story about five boa constrictors who killed their owner.

Finally, in spite of Paula's silent injunction not to find another therapist, I was in such pain and rage that I returned to the mental health center and found myself a therapist who decided I had profound issues with separation. And, as much as she claimed not to like the approach, this new therapist, Linda, decided to use the fashionable James Mann model of time-limited psychotherapy. She granted me ten sessions before cutting me loose. The whole trauma played itself out once again. Just as I thought there was someone to help me, the feeling evaporated. She terminated with me, talking excessively and seductively in the last session about how attached she had become to me.

After ending therapy, I quit my job in spite of my husband's protest over the loss of income and we moved out of the area. Within a month I fell in love with a woman who was the spitting image of Linda. But that's another story.

Epilogue

In fact, the stories piled up for five more years until I found out about Sex and Love Addicts Anonymous. Four additional years passed before I came to understand that Marjory's betrayal of my trust in her authority was a perfect replica of a phenomenon society has a nasty little word for: incest.

Ruined

Suzanne Grieco

Earrings, and bracelets wrangling
As I pushed them across your wrist.
They never came off.
I would see your arm next to me, you over me.
Me pulling at those bracelets.
You, this man with more jewelry than me and
                    longer hair.
I left everything for you.
                    Then I found these little cells that
I didn't want to tell you about.
Little cells I thought might be
Exciting. Intimate.
A stupid feminine fantasy.
Michael, we did what we had to do.
We killed them.
Ruined. Scraped.
I emerge from some wild coma of weeks:
You did what you had to do.
You saved yourself.
                    I pick up pieces like carnage. Like centrifuge.
I stick them back to me.
Then I try to find the things I loved before
I had eyes only for bracelets entwining.
And everything
                    is in the wrong place
And I could kill you —
You, whose jewelry I hear, mocking music
And whose bitter hair I still wipe from my mouth.
                    What a scar.
                    I feel ruined.
                    And now I just
                    Pray.

Thoughts After a Rape

Chris Mandell

Strange to think I have been raped
only once;
it felt so familiar,
so similar to things I had hoped were unimportant,
things we do not call rape.

The rape that we call rape,
is only one rape,
a rape with perhaps more articulate rage
but still akin to all those vague rapes
that we do not call rape.

The rape that we call rape
has shown me those other rapes
I had thought were nothing.
I have named them now.
I know now that rape is nothing more
than ignorance of the sacred.

There are more rapes than we might suppose.

A Name and a Face

♥

Patti Tana

In the summer of 1982, a man I was dating raped me. Two months before the rape my husband had divorced me and I was unmarried for the first time in my adult life. Many people warned me that I would be vulnerable, but I never imagined I'd find myself with the sort of man I had run away from my whole life — a violent man like my father.

I had met the man three years before at a course in the local library. After that we'd wave to each other on the rare occasions we happened to meet in town. When we met in a gift shop that summer we were both feeling lonely and rejected from the recent breakup of our marriages. He lived next door to a friend of mine and invited both of us to a barbecue with our children. It seemed safe.

For the next few weeks we rode our bicycles together, worked in our gardens, had more cookouts. When I worried about walking in our neighborhood at night, he showed me the large knife he kept strapped to his ankle. Just before our divorce my husband had been attacked by muggers, so I was conscious of the danger in the streets. The knife seemed a practical response to a menacing reality, and made me view him as a protector. Fearful of sleeping in the house alone with my six-year-old son, I welcomed his staying late. After the second week we started having sex. I was delighted to feel the flush of excitement again; I was delighted to *feel* again.

He was a machinist, used to making the world fit his needs. He fixed the doorbell so it rang every time. He tightened my bicycle brakes and adjusted the back door so it would lock. When he brought over a few tools to keep in the kitchen drawer, I thought of a friend's warning about not letting a man put his shoes under my bed or he'd think he owned the whole house. But I was so glad to have help with repairing the inevitable mechanical breakdowns that I didn't want to think about how expensive his help might prove to be.

One night he brought my little boy a quarter he'd made with heads on both sides. His children were visiting him, so we made popcorn and took the TV out on the upstairs porch for our kids to watch. Having him there restored my sense of family life.

Looking back I see there were signs of his potential violence, and I also see that I did not interpret this information correctly because my needs obscured my judgment. He claimed he'd had some bad breaks, and his scars elicited my sympathy rather than my wariness. I realized he drank too much; sometimes he'd drink himself to sleep.

Though he kept himself tightly in check, I sensed anger beneath the surface. He became jealous and made insulting remarks when I warmly greeted an old friend. One evening about a week before the rape, he snapped his belt off in anger at my son's childishness — a shocking replay of my own childhood beatings. Quickly, before he could hit him, I swept the boy out of the room and made the man leave my house. But after his own teenagers assured me he had never struck them, I gave him another chance. He swore that he had no intention of hitting my son, only scaring him, and that it would not happen again. I wanted to believe him.

Although I have blamed myself for not reacting decisively to these warnings, now I am trying to understand how it happened. And I am sharing this story to alert other women: if you sense *any* danger, be careful about giving second chances.

One day when I dropped off my son at his father's apartment for a visit, he said he wanted to discuss moving back home. I had never wanted him to leave in the first place. The man I was dating knew it, so when I saw him again, I told him I didn't want to go out with him anymore because I hoped to have a reconciliation. I had gathered the things he had left around the house (records, tools, an extra shirt), but he became angry when I tried to make him take them.

He said he wanted to sit on the porch for a few minutes. Although I desperately wanted him to leave before my son and former husband arrived, I tried to placate him. I poured some juice and went upstairs to join him on the second-floor porch.

He had turned over a small redwood table and was carving

letters into the underside with his knife. As he talked, he alternated between pointing the knife at me to punctuate his words and jabbing it into the wood with hard stabbing motions: "I want to fuck you one more time....You owe it to me."

At first I tried to reason with him. I explained that my mind and body were now oriented toward my former husband — surely he couldn't want to have sex with me when I didn't want it. But the more I reasoned, the angrier he became.

Now he was shaking the knife in my face as he repeated his demand. Glancing down I saw he had carved "I LOVE" into the wood. I feared that if I named what was happening — rape — he might drop the pretense that the knife in his hand was for stabbing the table and stab me.

I felt I had only as much time to think as it would take him to finish carving in the phrase. Should I jump off the high second-floor porch and maybe break a leg, or try to trick him and run outside to a neighbor? I could have screamed and perhaps attracted someone's attention before he stopped me, but I was petrified of provoking him.

I was also afraid he would come back if he didn't get what he wanted. Even if the police intervened in this instance because of the knife, I knew they could not keep him away from me in the future. I had to make him leave before my husband arrived to avoid a confrontation. There were no good alternatives. I decided to comply with his demand, hoping it would really be a "last time."

I felt my defenses were meager, but I tried to protect myself as much as I could. I needed a time limit so I lied and said my mother was due to arrive in a few minutes and I would have to call her to delay her visit. I reached through the open window for the phone in my bedroom, telling him he could listen to my conversation. When I called, she understood the lie and asked if I was alone. "No," I told her, "____ is here now, but he will be gone by seven. You should be here by seven." Now at least someone would know he was with me in case he injured me and I couldn't call for help — and *he* knew it too.

He stood outside the bathroom while I put in my diaphragm. Through the window I could hear neighborhood sounds — surely he would not kill me with so many people nearby.

It was just after six when we went into the bedroom. As he undressed I secretly turned the clock ahead a few minutes, but the hands still moved with excruciating slowness.

When I saw his knife by his pants on the floor, I kicked it under the bed so he could not get to it easily.

Though we'd been having sex for two weeks, now his body failed to respond to his will; he couldn't achieve an erection. That increased his anger. When I tried to help him so we could get it over with, he ordered me to lie on my back and not to touch him. The more frustrated he became, the more frightened I felt.

Finally he tensed his body enough to enter me, but it was grueling for both of us. At one point a girl in the street gave a loud laugh, breaking his concentration long enough for him to curse her. I was most terrified when he opened his tightly closed eyes and stared as if he didn't know who he was looking at. I thought he might blindly strangle me or smash my face. His stare was so distant and fierce that I said his name a few times and told him who I was. Again he told me to shut up and kept on pumping to ejaculation.

When he went to the bathroom, I grabbed the knife from under the bed, dressed quickly, and ran downstairs. I waited by the door. When he came down, he grumbled that the clock in the kitchen was ten minutes slower than the one by the bed. I shrugged. Then I handed him the knife as he left — I didn't want him coming back for it.

My mother arrived a few minutes later. Even then I could not bring myself to say that I had been raped. Instead I told her, "That was as close to rape as I ever want to come." She held my shaking body as I spoke.

I was relieved to be alive and grateful that I could walk and talk and breathe, but very afraid that he would return. I also felt my own limitations in a sickening way. Like so many other women who have been overpowered, I felt that a truck had run over me. Now I understood the desperate compromises people have to make. I was trying not to feel humiliated, to see that the shame was his and there was no excusing his actions. I did not blame myself for being raped, but I did feel fragile and foolish and broken and enraged.

Many other women's stories had taught me that the legal system reflects society's attitude that a woman loses her right to say no to a man after she once has said yes. In fact, much of my rage came from feeling trapped not only by the knife but by this lack of protection. Even if I had managed to escape from that particular situation, I was certain that my family and I would live in fear of future attacks because the police would not protect us.

I was so convinced that the police would just dismiss me, and so fearful that the rapist would take revenge on me for reporting him, that it took my friends nine days to convince me to report to the police. I decided to file the complaint to establish grounds for an order of protection in case he returned. I also realized that I owed it to other women.

Two male officers listened to what I had to say, made notes, and ran a computer check to see if he had a criminal record. They said the district attorney would probably not pursue the case but that they could go to the rapist's house and "scare" him. I told them not to. They assured me that if he were to appear at my home again I should call them and they would respond.

Four months after the rape, my friend who was his neighbor informed me that the man had moved.

But for years he stayed in my nightmares. Now I am less trusting of men — and of my own judgment. I no longer list the phone in my name. I no longer open my door to strangers. And my memories of that summer are slashed by the image of the knife.

For years I kept the table with "I LOVE" carved underneath to remind me of how people confuse love and possession, love and domination, love and rape. While I was being raped I did not dare name what was happening to me. Afterward, a friend who was helping me sort out my feelings said, "Now rape has a name and a face." Though I am still sometimes afraid, by writing about this rape I am naming what he did to me.

Leaves

Nancy Lott Gauld

A slammed door and silence.
Everywhere but in my head.
In there I still hear echoes
replaying the angry words.
Across the river
an April wind
twists the budding treetops.
I feel like the trees.
Bent, buffeted, unprotected.
Longing for a warmer climate,
a gentler touch.
If only feelings
could be more like leaves.
Able to right themselves
immediately
whenever the wind stops blowing.

Stripped Surrender

💔

Caitlin Morrell

nerves woven tightly into an opaque sheet
fray with every sound from his mouth
wants and needs unravel her sanity.
soon harsh eternities of silence
strip her emotions ragged,
sensuality slips off the edge.
the minds and bed are bare,
but bodies mechanically weave
a loose, translucent reality
to cover the loss of feeling.

Sentiment for All Seasons

Joanne Seltzer

Last Rosh Hashana
the rabbi
sermonized
on how much it hurts
when birthdays
and anniversaries
are disregarded
and I thought
yes it does hurt.

I had just had
a fight with Stan
and one of my complaints
was that birthdays
and anniversaries
are nothing to him
and that I
have been nothing
for years.

So when Stan gave me
a contemporary
sexy-wifey
birthday card
I thanked him politely
though I felt
neither happy

nor grateful
but merely bitter.

If a woman
has to beg
for a birthday card
or has to beg
for sex
by the time
she gets it
she won't want it
anymore.

The Stain

💔

Vickie C. Posey

"Now," he says as he comes toward her holding a spoon he's just lifted from the silverware drawer. "How could anyone in their right mind put this spoon away as if it were clean?"

He talks in generalities when he wants to point out some deficiency on her part. Not, "How could *you*," but, "How could *anyone*."

"In *his or her* right mind," she mumbles almost inaudibly beneath her breath.

"What?"

"Nothing."

She looks at the spoon he holds before her. Indeed it is covered with what she supposes is dried egg from a scrambled egg sandwich she made for Teri.

He hates eggs. She doesn't cook them when he's around. Must have been Monday when he was out of town.

She takes the spoon from him and turns toward the sink. It is a running battle, this. He thinks she should wash the dishes before she puts them in the dishwasher. She thinks it's silly to have a dishwasher if you have to wash the dishes anyway. And anyway, she thinks, which is more important, dried egg on a tiny tablespoon or a pronoun antecedent agreement? He makes many agreement errors in his speech; sometimes it drives her crazy. At other times, she feels a weird satisfaction just knowing he is making a mistake yet oblivious to it. She never mentions it directly to him, because she never knows what his reaction might be. Sometimes when she responds, he erupts, almost hitting her, yet stopping short. He would not want to be known as a man who hits women. Which is worse, dried egg on a spoon or agreement errors? It is a question she will ponder while he's away on another trip.

"Fluffy did it," she jokes as she scrubs the spoon with a scouring pad. She looks over her shoulder to Teri, her five-year-old daughter, who has come into the kitchen for breakfast. Teri giggles.

"While I was out," she whispers to Teri, "Fluffy jumped up on the counter, stuck her paw into the sink, got the dirty spoon and put it in the drawer. Just to get me in trouble."

Teri giggles again. Her father reads the paper silently.

She's trying to handle the situation with care, like she's read about in *I'm OK, You're OK*. The author says that people act like either parents, adults or children. Her first reaction had been to shove the spoon down his throat. Her second had been to say, "If it bothers you, then wash it." As she pours herself a cup of coffee, she tries to analyze her reactions. The first is probably childish, but the second seems pretty okay. She thinks the book would approve. What she knows, however is that this latter reaction would not be okay with her husband. It would make him even more infuriated than if she tried to shove the spoon down his throat.

At times, she can see his point, the point he reminds her of time and time again. Since he's making all the money, away most of the time doing his job, the least he should expect is to pick up a spoon and have it be free from dried egg. The problem is that it isn't just the dried egg. It's everything, as though she's always trying to pass some sort of test. Are the spoons clean enough, is she thin enough, does Teri brush her teeth enough? When he is away it is much easier. Then she can just settle down and be herself. She hates to admit that she sometimes looks forward to his leaving.

Finally, she sits down at the table, folds her hands around the warm coffee cup and lifts it to her mouth. Teri has gotten a box of Fruit Loops from the cupboard and is pouring some into her bowl.

"Can't you fix her something decent to eat?" he says. "And could I please have a spoon?"

She winces and starts to speak, but instead gets up and walks toward the silverware drawer. No use causing a scene now. He'll be gone soon and things will be calm. She lifts out one spoon and examines it carefully. When she hands it to him, he holds it up to the light and looks first at one side, then another. Finally he uses it to stir his coffee.

Relieved that the spoon passed the inspection, she sits down once more and sips her coffee, strong and black. He always makes the coffee, first carefully washing the pot, then grinding fresh beans.

He is precise in measuring both coffee and water. Later, after the brewing is completed, at the manual's suggestion, he stirs the coffee to give it extra flavor. She smiles and sips. He really does make a great cup of coffee.

"I need to be at the airport at 8:30," he says as he turns the last page of the newspaper.

She will take him as she usually does. He doesn't ask her if she has time; he just assumes she will be there when he needs to go. It's easier for him if she takes him, no parking and lugging bags across the parking lot.

"OK, Teri, let's go get on our clothes and brush our teeth."

She clears the table. Later, in their bedroom she pulls on some warm-up pants and laces up her running shoes while her husband, clad in wing-tip shoes, dress pants and shirt, stands erect before the full-length mirror. As he works his tie into place, she watches this man she has lived with for fifteen years. She seems not to know him now, not at all like she once did, or thought she did. Sometimes she wonders if he is capable of loving anybody. She wonders, as she often does lately, if she loves him. She can't decide. As he pulls on his coat, she notices a tiny stain, just a speck, on the back of his shirt collar. It's a truly small stain, hardly noticeable to most, but still evident above his jacket. Amazing that he didn't catch it before he put on his shirt, she thinks. He had sent many a shirt back to the cleaners for less.

She starts to point it out, but decides against it. He'd change shirts and she'd have to make another trip to the cleaners. And besides she finds some joy in thinking that he will sit in first class, later perhaps lunch with important people in a fancy restaurant, with a stain on his collar.

As they ride to the airport, she debates whether she should tell him. She feels guilty watching him from the side as he sits straight, adjusting his tie from time to time. *He believes he is so perfect,* she thinks. *Should I tell him he's not?*

"Can you pay the phone bill, please," he says. "Last month, the payment was late."

"Sure."

At the airport, he leans over to give her a quick kiss. She smells his aftershave and feels his smooth face against hers.

He turns to his daughter and throws her a kiss. It would wrinkle him too much to reach over the seat to kiss her. And besides, she knows he worries about Teri's sticky hands touching him if he gets too close.

"Bye sweetie," he says to his daughter.

"Have a good trip," she says as he turns to open the door. Again she sees the stain. As he opens the trunk to get his bags, she rolls down the window and looks back at him.

"Wait a second," she says.

"Can't" he says without any hesitation. "Gotta go. See you Friday."

She watches as he checks his airline ticket once more. He walks away and waves goodbye.

That night she and Teri will have scrambled eggs and bacon for dinner. Tomorrow morning they plan to have peanut butter and jelly sandwiches.

Bone

Renee A. Ashley

The stepchild eats you until you are raw, are bone. He
spits out the ragged pieces he has gnawed at the feet
of his true parent. He is saying: "You want this?
Take it. Here it is. Meat, bits of meat. See what I
Leave you? Bone."

Then the parent loves the bone, loves the bone, says oh
how you suffered for me, how I love you, love you.
Look at what he has done, oh, oh, oh. Then the parent
devours the bone, whole, and is alone, as he must have
wished, with the child.

how it feels with half the loaf

💔

s.l. wisenberg

your friends say, "it is only half a loaf,
surely you must realize that."
you say: "but i am not all that hungry."
you say: "but it really is a big half,
you know. The biggest half...i have, for example,
in my not-so-few years, rarely seen a halfloaf
as large. it is quite extraordinary,
this halfloaf. i must save it. though perhaps it is magical,
do you think that could be? perhaps it grew
from a crumb, it will never diminish, it is under a spell
of some kind,
like the keg that supplies endless rounds of beer
in fairy tales with morals like: you must trust
the source of your bounty."

"but it is not bounty we're talking about," your friends say.
"we are looking at its opposite. we are talking about
settling for
less. scarcity.
we are talking about blinding yourself with the whiteness
of the loaf, of chanting, 'it is enough, it is enough.
oh so plenty. i am satisfied.' we are talking about hypnotizing
the self, the part of the self
that hungers most."

you cover your ears, you answer:
"this halfloaf is better
than what i see all around. this is as much as i can

spend. i cannot loose my fingers from it.
i cannot afford to let it go
into the wind.
i cannot leave my hearth
and seek better. i cannot afford to leave this halfloaf behind
though now i admit it is becoming ragged and i am afraid
to bite in with gusto
for the usual reasons.
i have forgotten the way it tastes. i was afraid to enjoy it
too deeply, afraid of never getting my fill.
fear bit into me."

your friends, now stern: "you must drop it drop it on the ground.
now. you must forget it. you must set your sights higher. you
must believe —"

"but where is a full loaf?" you ask. "i have no guarantee that
anything else would sate me. do you? how fresh, how full are
your own loaves?" you ask. angry. "full enough," one or two
retort.

the others add: "we are seeking, seeking, at this moment. we are
stretching our jaws. flexing our stomachs. join us. look up
ahead. there is much promise."

you follow their eyes:
nothing over the horizon
but the haze of a hunger.

The Concert Master

♥

Barbara M. Simon

You can't trust him
there in black
on the stage, the orchestra behind him,
the violin coming alive to his touch.
He sways
in an ecstasy of motion
to the music he bleeds like passion
from wood. The audience follows
his fine hands, the hands
that slap like cymbals,
knock you around,
send you ass over tincups
around the room, down the stairs
without sound. There's no music there.
You wake one Thursday,
jaw bruised, eye black.
"Don't take him back," your sister says.
"Screw the bastard!" advise your friends.

You hate him.
Rage ringing like brass in your heart,
you decide to face him down,
tell him what you think.
Before your wrath, he bows,
begs you
to play out your anger
as if he were tympani.

Of course you can't. Because
just as you begin
to rap out
the rhythm of your rage
you recall
how his fine hands once moved,
played down your back
and you made only low notes,
the tone of your longing
lovely as a cello:
music without words,
your desire
the perfect symphony he composed.

MAN!

Nancy Izawa

He wants me
When I'm
Standing tall
Looking fine
Acting sassy

Then he
Puts me down
Laughs me down
Brings me down
Wears me down
Knocks me down

So I
Stand up tall
Wipe my tears
Turn around
And walk away.

Now
He wants me
Back.

MAN!

Vines

Mary Crescenzo Simons

I stand on the bottom rung
while your ankles, pink and dry,
ascend before my eyes
to tame the ivy, wild and rising
from the ground
of this ancient house.

Asked to be the weight,
the balance and the anchor
for your trip to the upper floors,
I dodge falling branches,
staring beyond the aluminum rods
to windows of a kitchen door
smudged with your prints
that steal light.

Fluted bars squeak
as you begin your descent,
clippers securely in hand,
and I debate the right moment
to step aside,
not knowing how
to release the extension
without having you fall.

breaking
the Spell

The Past

Lynn Leone

Aint no man gonna take away
My heart and soul
And whip me with it.

Chronicle of Violence

💔

Marie Cartier

I don't owe you anything. You slap me, push me against the wall,
hold my face down smothering me, spit on me, break china in my
kitchen, break down my door, threaten to kill my cat, slash my
tires, bust up my place. You take away all the gifts you've
given me, sleep with other women, then lie about it. Wake me up
in the middle of the night. Tell me I'll go crazy like my
sister. I have the cops in and you call me a victim. You say I
must like getting hit or I wouldn't be here....I hate it.

You don't understand. You say I like to be hit. You don't
understand.

I'm searching. You call, your voice sweet honey. Babe, you say, I
miss you. I want you. I love you. I begin to melt
again, your arms, your hair on my shoulder. Again your hands
rubbing my shoulders. Again and then again. *Yes.* I love you,
too, I say, finally. Forgetting. Not caring. If...was it even
you that slapped me open-handed? Told me you wished my mother
would die? Was it you? It couldn't be you. Now, on the phone,
telling me I'm beautiful, you're crazy about me. Was it you
or,...was it...someone else? I need to know these things. I ask this
question because I need to know. I'm forgetting.

I'm forgetting how you banged my head against the wall, my
barrette breaking, my hair flying around my face like china. Like
the cup you threw at my wall, followed by the vase, the red wax
shattering...skidding across the floor. Was it you who knocked
me from my seat, then slapped me when I tried to stand? I ask

this question, because I *need* to know. I'm forgetting.

I'm forgetting. I was a battered woman.
...I was a battered woman.

never again
Never, never again.

Now Look What You Have Done

Cheryl Townsend

I've been left
alone to miss you
so many times now
that I just don't
anymore

Flashbacks

❣

Elayne Clift

I

Tall and erect, with salt-and-pepper hair growing erratically toward dark, deep-set eyes. Tweedy and unkempt, attractive in an Englishman. He follows her, moving from one gallery to the next, his appreciation of art overpowered, she knows, only by curiosity about herself, a young woman in a red raincoat. Later, while sipping amontillado sherry together at the Chandos Bar off Trafalgar Square, he confesses. "It was the raincoat. And that you were alone. That's why I never took you for American."

"I suppose you think all American women have long blonde hair, California tans, and London Fogs?" she teased. "And travel in droves."

"Something like that."

Easy talk. Real talk. Past the preliminaries, and still a hint of secrets kept. Rain pellets on the window making the Chandos nook with its chintz bench cushions and brass rubbings feel like home. Sherry warming the body.

"I wish I could take you to dinner, but I've got a bloody plane to catch back up north."

"Never mind. I'll walk you to the tube."

The hint of moisture in the air hovering like thin fog after a rain. Arms touching as long strides make up for lost minutes. Past the Cavell monument, across the wet square to Charing Cross station. Then a kiss, a glance that makes talking moot, and like a scene from a World War II movie, he disappears into the bowels of British Rail. A curious rending, and in three hours, all of life has changed.

II

"Checking out today, then?"

"Yes. I'm going on to Paris."

"Well, you'll need a good breakfast. Oh, I nearly forgot. There's a letter for you." The plump Italian woman hands over an envelope and smiling, hurries off to the kitchen while her dour English husband scowls over his accounts. The small dining room with its flowered wallpaper and white embroidered tablecloths begins to fill up with tourists seduced from their rooms by the smell of fried bacon and eggs. It is a pleasant enough bed-and-breakfast.

"The Queen's Court, 182 Inverness Rd., Bayswater, London." The handwriting is an unfamiliar graceful scrawl, the postmark York. Whoever...and then inaudibly, Oh! She opens the blue envelope with a peculiar sensation in her stomach.

"It's never happened to me before, please believe that. Meeting you has done something quite extraordinary. I can't stop thinking of you. So there are things I must tell you..."

Why does the wife matter? It's not really a surprise, not even that it's a poor marriage. One could have easily guessed — the loose references to "we," the office address instead of home. They'll never meet again. It was just an infatuation, something to make a first European journey more memorable. Funny, the sense of loss she feels. Still a reply is in order. Acknowledgement. Closure.

And so the correspondence is begun.

III

It goes on for nearly a year, until the letters become central to their lives. Although she returns to the States, through the written word, they grow intimate. "My dearest darling," his letters begin. She attempts restraint. "Dearest Derek." There is something unnatural in the deepening knowledge of each other across the sea, without touch or sight; this wants watching. But she hungers for the letters, devours them when they come, begins to plan her return. He encourages her, longingly and passionately, even as he reminds her that under the circumstances, the decision must be hers. She makes it freely, she says, to live abroad as she has always wanted to do. He is the catalyst, not the cause, she tells him, embracing the delusion almost as much as he does, and in the spring, she is on a ship carrying her eastward on a sea swelling with possibility.

IV

He comes aboard to greet her and the sight of him catches her breath. He is taller, older, nattier than she remembered. She knows that tonight she will sleep with him, and he is suddenly a stranger. *What have I done?* she thinks. Why am I here? But then his arms are around her, his breath warm on her neck, his long, lean body fitting against her own slenderness as if it were meant to be there and the year and the sea and the questions between them dissolve. Nothing matters but their togetherness, no matter what it will cost them. As they leave the ship, the purser calls after her, "Hello, Miss! Letter for you. Just brought on board. You nearly missed it!" On the envelope the now-familiar script that has become her lifeline. They laugh, and he kisses her full and warm and long on the mouth. "Never mind about that now," he says, grinning broadly, and leads her to his car and a two-week holiday in Cornwall, so idyllic, so loving, that she has no idea of the price to be paid.

They lie side-by-side in the inn at Dorchester and watch through a skylight dormer as daylight intrudes. Their lovemaking has been good; full and rich and kind. They are deeply satisfied. She nestles into the side of his long body, warm and welcoming and he strokes her face. "Imagine," she says with the hint of a giggle. "Five o'clock in the morning and we're actually talking to each other. I can't believe it won't take five days to know what you're thinking."

"You'll always know what I'm thinking my darling."

And on this, their first morning, she has no reason to wonder.

The days in Cornwall are languid, abundant with English treasures. They awake lazily, make love in a room full of seaside sounds and smells. Crisp white window curtains flap in the breeze like sheets hung out to dry. The chill of salt air makes them huddle together, and only the smell of breakfast and appetites made ravenous by heightened senses force them from their nest. After breakfast, they stroll to the quayside to watch the fishing boats bobbing in the harbor, then up the hill to the stone church and on to the village center.

After lunch they visit neighboring villages, one more beautiful than the next in their Lilliputian settings. In Mevighessy they eat cockles and mussels fresh from the sea, in Lerryn they sip bitter in the pub while a group of men, local bellringers, sing "Little Jimmy Brown" a cappella and it is so beautiful she cannot keep from weeping. "Why are you crying?" he asks. "Because I'm so happy, and the rest of the world is so sad," she replies.

In the evenings they cross from Polruan to Fowey on the foot ferry to visit the pubs there and listen to ballads in Gaelic. She is a novelty, this American in the red raincoat, and he smiles as the locals ask what brought her here. She and Derek play darts and dance if there's music.

One day they go to Devon, near the moors to meet an old army buddy in The King George. The huge fireplace welcomes them against the chill of an afternoon rain. After a while, fire and friendship warm them. The friend is called Tom, his wife Diana, they are good people and never ask how it came to be that the two of them are there together. It feels good to have friends. "I hope we see you again," she says. Diana smiles. Afterwards he tells her, "Tom told me in the men's room, how lucky I was to have you. Things aren't going very well between him and Diana."

And then as they knew it must, the holiday ends and they drive back to London together. He drops her off at The Queen's Court where she will stay once again until she can find a flat and begin her new job. She tries desperately to be cheerful, not to weep at the parting. She has promised herself never, ever to ask more of him than he has offered to give. Still, his farewell seems a bit cavalier. "Bye, bye, Darling! See you in a few weeks. Cheerio!"

V

The first weeks are lonely. She is busy with moving to the West End flat she has found to share with two other professional women, and with starting her new job as an editor for the magazine group she left in New York, but mostly she thinks about him, wonders what he is doing in the evenings, why he can't manage to call. It would be difficult, of course, from home. Still he often goes to the office to write her long, effusive letters. "I long for you. You are my only happiness. I cannot imagine life without you anymore." After a while the letter she has most wanted to see comes. "I will be in London next month. We can have a long weekend away. I count the days."

She also counts, and by the time he arrives, she is trembling with anticipation. They set off late on a Friday evening for Coventry, Banbury and Warwick Castle, hungry for all that can be packed into the three days granted them by his business travel. Neither is disappointed. The English countryside is Constable unfrozen from canvas; they are Barrett and Browning come to life. Their time together is so exquisitely pleasurable that it becomes nearly painful, and when the time comes for parting, she feels her soul shrunken as if it had been seared by a branding iron. He too is sad, but his equilibrium seems curiously untouched. *So unlike a woman,* she thinks.

And so the pattern is soon established: every month or six weeks a rendezvous. Vivid, extraordinary moments, stretched out and packed into three days in the Midlands, or Salisbury or Cambridge or Canterbury. Once he even meets her in York, taking her on a pub crawl dangerously close to home, showing her off to the few friends and colleagues who have his confidence about his "American girlfriend." And always it is the same. Passionate, rich and full, with melancholy intruding as gatekeeper when their time is up. Once they fly to the west coast of Ireland where he (and his wife) own a cottage by the sea. He makes love to her in the bed where his wife still sleeps when she is there. Afterward, she opens a drawer and finds a woman's sweater and she feels ashamed. "I don't want to come here again," she says. He touches her arm. "Don't be silly, Darling," he says. "She hasn't been here with me in two years."

Once, on one of their weekends, he seems distant, preoccupied. She watches him climb a heather-covered hill and stand, a solitary figure, on a precipitous cliff at the top. She feels frightened, not only of what would happen if he fell, but beyond that. Fear grips her stomach and chest in a way she does not understand and she wants to shout at him, "Come down! Come down!" but her voice is frozen within her, and she knows that he would not come anyway. He turns and waves at her, and even though she cannot see his face, she knows that he is grinning.

Later in the night he turns from her, pulling her towards him from behind. "Don't ever leave me," he pleads suddenly. "Promise me you won't ever leave me." "I won't leave you," she says, putting the blanket around him, despite her own chill because giving is in her nature. And because taking is in his, he pulls the blanket's warmth, and hers, around him, and sinks into sleep.

The weeks that pass now between their times together grow more difficult for her. Their weekends become respite for the long, lean days and nights without him, when life seems shallow and unconnected to reality. She tries to immerse herself in all that London can offer, but it is empty. Quietly she craves her old job, where she was valued and excited far above what the new workplace allows. And she wonders why for him, it seems so easy. For the first time, she begins to ponder the future, and questions till now repressed break through her consciousness. And of these, the loudest is *When?*

One day Tom, the old army buddy, comes to London and rings her for lunch. They meet at the pub close to her office. "It's wonderful to see you," he says like an old and dear friend. "And you," she replies. "I really enjoyed that day in Devon. How's Diana?" "Oh, you know, it's lonely down there. She isn't very happy really. It's not like you and Derek. God, it must be wonderful to be that much in love." She smiles, sad for him and for Diana and for herself. "Why not bring her to London," she offers. "Maybe the four of us could have a weekend." But she knows they never will.

Soon after, she calls Derek who is coming in two weeks. "I saw Tom," she says. "We had lunch. He's such a nice man. I'm sorry about him and Diana." After a long pause he says, "Yes, well, there you are. Anyway, I'll be there Friday week. God, I'm longing to see you."

On the Friday he is due, she waits from eleven o'clock in the morning to hear that he has arrived, but the call doesn't come until just before five. "Where've you been? I've been worried," she tells him. "I got in late. I'll meet you at the office at half five." She hears the tension in his voice and feels a paralyzing chill creep up her stomach to her chest. She sees it in his face when she races down to the lobby, wild with longing, to meet him. They go to the pub, the same one where she and Tom had lunch, and order drinks. "I've been dying to see you," she says, taking his hand. "What's wrong?" "How long have you been sleeping with Tom?" he asks, his black eyes flashing rage at her like a demented stranger.

She wants to scream, to throw beer in his face, to run for her life across the road into the park until, gasping for breath, she can cling to a tree for support. She wants him to follow her and she wants to claw his eyes out. But instead, frozen to the seat, she hears the sound of her own sobbing and realizes that her chest is heaving and she cannot breathe.

"Let's get out of here," he says, leading her past the tables of staring patrons, some of whom know her from the office. In a trance, she reaches the hotel they have booked, her mind racing and stumbling as if it were chased by a herd of wild animals. "How could you say that? How could you think it?" she hears herself say over and over again. "Don't you realize what a good friend Tom is. Don't you know how much I love you. Have you got any idea how much he envies us?" And while the stunned questions spill out, a piece within rages quietly, so deep, so untapped that it is almost imperceptible, overpowered by a curious sense of calm and kindness which has begun to settle over her like exhaustion.

"I'm sorry, oh my God, I'm sorry," he pleads like a lost child. "I love you. I love you so much I go mad sometimes. I began to imagine all sorts of things when you told me you'd seen him. Christ, I'm so sorry. I must be crazy. Please, please, forgive me." He smothers her with kisses, wiping her eyes, pushing her hair out of her face. They collapse on the bed and hold each other as if it were a fragile sailboat in a squall, and as dusk overtakes them, she falls into the fitful sleep of a feverish child. When she awakens, he is sitting in the chair watching her. He smiles tentatively. As she begins to rise, a fly buzzes past her face, and she sees for the first time that the hotel room they are in is shabbily lit and slightly sordid.

VI

"I don't feel I can go on like this much longer," she finally tells him on one of their London weekends. (They are less inclined to go to the countryside now, as if they had run out of places, and fantasies.) "It's not just us. It's my work. My life. Where's it all going?" "You knew what the situation was when you came here," he says. "It was your choice. I never asked you. I never said I would want to leave my wife and marry again. I'm not cut out for it. There were no conditions for either of us. We just wanted to be together. Besides, you said you were coming for lots of other reasons." In the end she knows it is futile to discuss it and slowly, slowly, she lets the knowledge of what she must do wash over her. When she is certain, she says, "I'm leaving. There's nothing else to be done. I must leave." "Perhaps it would be best," he says.

VII

Years later, when she could think about it sanely, rationally and truly understand him and herself, she saw that she had in her an instinct for emotional survival so strong that it enabled her to go. But at the time, it was the weakness that precedes death that allowed her to go through the necessary motions of leaving. And even through the packing and leave-taking, still they made time to make love like starving people clinging to scraps of sustenance. And even in the last moment, she supposed because none of it had ever seemed real, she went through the motions with dignity and grace. Only later, much later, when they sealed the airplane door like the lid of a coffin, did she let go and give way to a grief so deep, so wrenching, so pervasive, that she felt even months and years later as though every organ of thinking and feeling and being in her body had been surgically excised.

VIII

Afterwards there were a few letters at first, then only Christmas cards. He came once to America on business, long after she was married and had children, and of course he called. And as always, she could not resist him, so she agreed to meet him between flights, partly out of curiosity, partly vindication.

He looked old, balding and gray-haired, but the grin was familiar, the suit still natty tweed. They talked, remembered — he with crystal clarity, she impressionistically. "So much of what you told me turned out to be right," he said. "I am alone, just as you predicted. I'll never forget your saying that to me in a pub one night: 'You'll grow old alone, unloved. You'll regret your choices one day.'" "Did I say that?" "That and a lot more. You taught me so much. But most of all, the love of a woman for a man. I've never forgotten and I never found it like that anywhere else. Still, I have no regrets. We had such a special time together, didn't we?" She nodded, rising to leave. "And now you're happy. Married to a good man. Nice children. Just as it should be." "Yes," she said. "Just as it should be."

She felt his eyes on her until she could no longer have been in his view. Perhaps that was why she held her head high and light, which was also how she felt. Cleansed. Intact. Well balanced and firm of foot. It had been necessary to come. Acknowledgement. Closure. And so it was ended, and life went on, unchanged yet ever changing.

Elegy for the Other Woman

💔

Elisavietta Ritchie

May her plane explode
with just one fatality.
But, should it not,
may the other woman spew
persistent dysentery from
your first night ever after.
May the other woman vomit
African bees and Argentine wasps.
May cobras uncoil from her loins.
May she be eaten not
by something dramatic like lions,
but by a warthog.
I do not wish the other woman
to fall down a well
for fear of spoiling the water,
nor die on the highway because
she might obstruct traffic.
Rather: something easy, and cheap,
like clap from some other bloke.
Should she still survive
all these critical possibilities,
may she quietly die of boredom with you.

Chains

❣

Ellen E. Behrens

It has been plaguing her for weeks now, this smell of decay in the apartment. So she cleans and cleans, spending hours in the bathroom rubbing the faucets and basins until they reflect her face and she leans away, stoops to reach under the sink to sort out soaps and dust the curve of the pipes. Still, the scent of the nearly dead lingers.

Now she lies, exhausted, in bed, her eyes tracing familiar patterns, her ears trying not to hear occasional cars pass the building. She tries not to wait for the sound of tires on the gravel driveway. She tries to think of what she's accomplished today, imagines a list forming in her head: bathroom tub including tile, disinfected. Kitchen floor, waxed.

The cleaning exhausts her, but there is something else, too, pulling down inside her like a metal weight. Sometimes she lets her fingers caress her stomach, a light massage, a gentle stroking. She imagines the weight is an anchor that lowers inside her, slowly, gentle in its way, but oh so heavy. Sometimes she falls asleep like this, her hands feeling for the spot where the weight is, inside, but she never finds it.

Tonight she thinks of calling someone and imagines a different list, a list of names with pictures and faces. She wonders who to call: Marie, no. Suzanne, no. The digital clock clicks and she knows a West Coast call is the only kind that would make sense at this hour, so she dials. "Hi, Jen," she says when the voice of her old roommate answers. "It's Natalie."

"God, Nat! How are you? Is something wrong?"

"Oh, no," she says, "not at all," but the words feel like a lie. It takes her a second to realize that so much, anymore, is a lie. She knows already she'll say Daniel's out of town and she's lonely — only the part about being lonely the truth.

She can see, in her mind, Jen on the other end of the phone, busy cooking or doing a crossword or stitching some alteration to an outfit from Salvation Army that'll look sensational only on Jen. Jen who never compromises what she's set out to do — not for anything, not even for a long-distance call at 2 a.m. EST.

"So what's up?" Jen has asked and she rattles off a list — being in charge of setting up the new store at Great Oaks Mall tops it. She remembers to ask Jen about her job and, too soon, she thinks, hears, "How's Daniel, anyway?"

"He's fine."

This is when the image hits: his thighs, strong from jogging and tennis, wrapped around slender legs. The curled initial at the end of that note she found, the note she'd crumpled and hurled into the room somewhere. She's tried so hard to not imagine them as flesh and blood, as blonde or brunette, as having needs and wants — as having her husband while she sits alone. She's tried so hard to convince herself it will all be over soon, with this one, and then there won't be another. She tries not to think of how many times she's hoped for the end.

There's a giggle in her ear and at first she thinks it's the note, an aural surging of mockery, and then she realizes that of course it's Jen. "Your honeymoon must be over, finally, it only lasted, what, five years?" Jen is saying. "I would have thought you'd have better things to do at — what, two a.m. your time?"

"He's out with someone," she says, the words surprising her more than they surprise Jen, she's sure.

"You're kidding, right? You don't mean another woman."

The note hadn't even revealed this to her. He had, when he'd come to her, sheepish, embarrassed, the look she later decided was like that of a school kid with a crush smeared all over his thirty-three-year-old face. There had been others, before this one, but they hadn't been worthy of his honesty, she supposed, because this time he'd asked her. What would she think, would she understand?

"Not Daniel," Jen is saying. "Something must have gone haywire with him."

In Jen's voice she hears that she would have been better off alone in this. She hears in the questions ("How do you know, Nat? Are you sure?") and the support ("I can't believe he would do this to you!") all of the answers she can't give: "He was honest with me. He told me there's this attraction between them. What were my choices? Sure I could've said no, but then I would have waited for it to happen, like it always had before. I would have gone through his pockets and wallet and list of long-distance numbers on the phone bill anyway. How would my life have been any different than it is now?"

"It's hard to explain, Jen," is all that she does say.

"Tell him to dump her or you cut him loose," Jen says.

"It's not that simple."

"Sure it is. You've got a life, Nat. You don't deserve to be delegated to distraction status."

"Distraction?" She'd always thought the initial on the note was the distraction. Jen makes her doubt this.

"Not even Daniel. You've got to even up the sides."

But evening up the sides, she thinks, wouldn't even make the battle a fair one. There's something else. The question of fighting anymore at all. "I've got to go, Jen. Thanks."

"Call me soon."

She lies back. She hears the tap—of the bathroom faucet and the clock beside her clicking the seconds of her life away like the dripping of water into the drain. Two...three...four...five... She tries not to think of Jen's simple advice. How does she see things so cut and dried? Seven...eight... She tries to concentrate on the shrivelling away of time, on pulling her cracking heart back together. A heart, she thinks, that's old fashioned, a red valentine with doilies and an arrow through it.

Twelve...thirteen...fourteen... The seconds click and the water drips, their rhythm off. She tosses the covers from her and trips in the dark, heading for the bathroom. The lights around the mirror flash and she feels frozen in a photograph, her reflection grabbing her, holding her still. She remembers a motel room in the Poconos, the afternoon of kissing and making out like teenagers and finally, giving in to each other. She remembers the water pistol fight, though she's forgotten where the weapons came from, what the plan of them had been originally. She sees again them hurdling furniture to get better aim, firing and reloading and drenching the bed in cold water, then checking out, laughing, because they knew they never could have slept in that bed, after that, the cold water soaked through to the mattress.

The face looking back at her is smiling, a twinge of happy memory, but she turns away before it reminds her that there haven't been many like that since. She pads in soft slippers to the bedroom again and sneaks into the bed, pretending he's there and she doesn't want to wake him.

When he comes in, the clock has ticked past four and she feigns sleep. His weight shifts onto the bed. "Baby," he says, but she holds her eyes closed. "I love you," he whispers, touching her hands where they clasp her stomach. She tries not to tighten them, squeezing away the tears.

She listens to the clock, to his breathing, feels his heart pounding. The apartment, in this deep dark, is still rotten to her. She wonders again at the source of it, recalls her mental list of the things she's cleaned and checked: furniture polished, carpets vacuumed, wastebaskets emptied, every piece of clothing and every bit of kitchen, bathroom and bedroom linen laundered, folded, tucked away. She lists until he sleeps. Then she realizes the rotting is inside of her.

I'm not losing Daniel after all, she thinks. I'm losing myself.

The room lightens into dawn with each click of the clock. She lies, watching seconds flash by, wondering if animals, trapped in pairs, lie peacefully linked, or if they gnaw at themselves and each other in their tortured need to be free. Yet she knows.

And the heavy weight, suspended inside her like a pendulum, comes loose. She feels it, under her fingers, thundering through her. She feels it, but cannot stop it.

In the early light, she smiles.

Too High a Proof

💔

Sharon F. Suer

It took me some time
to understand
why the mouthwash disappeared so quickly
why you put out the trash
each night before I returned —
my denial complementing yours.

With realization,
the inevitable confrontation
but you deftly fenced the issue;
thrusting promises to recriminations,
parrying anger for reconciliations,
bottles and cans as witness.
You were so smooth
when I threw you out; but you see

I've tried
walking in the dark before
trusting not to step
on the cockroaches
with my bare feet;
Now I turn on the lights.

Walking Wounded

💔

Norma Blair

Shuffling down the endless hall, I was half listening to Emily's chatter. The sutures in my stomach made me walk with the stilted gait of a recent surgery victim. Victim is the right word. I felt like a burnt offering. It was a routine pap smear. The next thing I knew, the good doctor had harpooned my cancerous cervix. Each small step was a fresh experience in deep, tearing pain. By my lights, I was more than justified in feeling extremely ungrateful to the inflictor of wounds.

At least I was rid of the metal pole on a heavy wheeled base that held the glucose bag that dripped its clear contents into my veins. The day before, a gently sloping wheelchair ramp had become an Olympic downhill course, with me snorting away in a mad attempt to keep up with the rolling pole. The anguish I felt at the idea of having the needle torn from the tender inner flesh of my wrist gave me added incentive. I puffed to a stop at the bottom. Exhausted, but safe, I hailed a passing nurse who bit back a smile while helping me up the ramp and back to my room.

Emily Miller, new friend and fellow inmate, was a cystostomy patient. She was forty years old but seemed younger. The illusion was enhanced by the springiness of her step and her casual disregard for the plastic bag that hung from her waist, half full of urine. The yellow liquid sloshed and gurgled as we moved down the hall. Imagine that, here she was, wearing her pee on the outside.

As we walked and talked, Emily was getting ahead again.

I made puffing noises, then croaked, "Wait up."

She waited, gazing at the polished floor, fully chastised.

I leaned against the wall and dared her to show me one doctor who hadn't inflicted agony in order to relieve pain.

"Come on Annie," she said, ignoring my challenge, "we've got five miles of halls left to do."

Walking slower, but talking just as fast she told me how her alcoholic husband, Ted, had left her on their sofa, her swollen leg packed in ice. In a drunken rage he had shoved her down a flight of stairs. The doctor ordered her to keep the leg elevated and very cold. Ted's job was to keep the ice packs coming.

She was to the part where she lay abandoned in lukewarm water. Six hours ago Ted had gone for a pack of cigarettes. Emily decided that when he finally did return, he would find her in the precise position as when he left. The soggy mess of wet towels would be mute testimony to his cruelty.

The telephone was within reach but she wasn't about to let him off that easily. She'd lay there until doomsday, dying slowly of starvation not to mention waterlogness. He was going to witness her misery if it killed her.

I knew the feeling. My husband, Frank, is an alcoholic, too. He hadn't been to the hospital to visit me and I knew why. He was on a bender. I wasn't surprised or even hurt. Not any more. I had even begun to suspect that I just might be part of the problem.

I had taken the second shift at the shoe factory because it meant more money. Then I was better able to make good on Frank's bouncing checks. I always explained or excused his behavior to family and friends. But now I was tired of the whole scene. I was seriously thinking of getting out of the marriage before my mouth got that look of a prune sucking a lemon.

Maybe it was this cancer, telling me that not only was I mortal, but in definite peril of buying the farm. It was the loss of self-esteem, too. The names he always ended up screaming at me, bitch, slut, whore. Or, maybe it was seeing myself mirrored in Emily. The way she pretended to be lighthearted and brave while keeping her alkie husband in booze and out of jail. Blaming herself for the cystostomy when it was the result of spinal cord damage. That had happened when Ted shoved her down the stairs. Ted hadn't been to see her, either.

Wanting to rest, I hotfooted it, if you can call taking teeny weeny steps, hotfooting, to my room. This was the third day after surgery. The nurses' collective attitude was that I should have been gliding the halls ballerina-like, or, failing that, at least twenty miles a day at a brisk waddle.

Doctor Westra had told me I was very lucky. Just the cervix, uterus and one ovary were removed. They had gotten all the cancer, he thought. I didn't feel so lucky.

I sat down gingerly on the edge of the bed and flipped up my nightie to inspect the wound. It was an ugly thing. The black stitches puckered my flesh like a row of fishhooks. The incision ran from hip to hip. The colors clashed, too — black, yellow, brown and a suffused orangish red.

I had never clapped eyes on Emily's hubby, but I knew him. Like Frank, Ted lied, cheated, accused. He would do anything to keep from being recognized as diseased. If that included pushing Emily down the stairs, he'd do it. Knowing which emotional circuits to trip is another symptom of alcoholism. When Frank accused me of whoring around, it didn't have to have a basis in fact. It was, however, a sure-fire ruse to keep me off balance, to keep the focus away from him.

"Anybody home?" Emily stood in the doorway looking lost.

"Yeah, come on in." I pulled my flaming red robe closed and carefully lay back on the bed.

"How long have you and Frank been married?" She asked shyly.

"Eight and a half too long years."

"Are you really going to divorce him?" There was something like fear on her face, as if it would be a personal loss to her if I said yes.

"Yes. I've been saving my money at the credit union at work."

Emily couldn't meet my eyes. "I wish I could be strong like you..." Her voice trailed away. She twisted her fingers.

"I don't feel strong. There's just got to be something better before I die. I guess that's it, really." I smiled at her, not knowing what else to say.

"Will you come and see me...after we get out...?" She looked like a hopeful child, expecting to be refused.

I felt sorry for Emily, but not as much as I might have only weeks before. I couldn't save her from herself. It was up to her to stop living through Ted.

The nurse with the juice and crackers had come and gone. Night in the hospital is not a likely place for log-sawing slumber. It was like trying to sleep on top of a building-sized machine, shifting from a frantic bustle to a subdued turmoil. It has the sensation of busyness no matter how they try to disguise it with dimmed lighting and rubber-soled shoes.

Morning came, and with it, a hardened resolve. Emily was going home today. I walked, with a lot less pain, to her room to say goodbye.

Emily looked just as small and frightened in her street clothes as she did in hospital issue.

"What'll your husband do to you?" Her eyes were wide with concern for me.

"I'm sure he'll accuse me of using him, recovering at home on his paycheck while I plot behind his back to leave him. He'll say I'm screwing the doctor. Cheerful little things like that. He'll probably hit me."

"You're really going to do it, aren't you?"

I nodded.

I went to the door. "Good luck to you, Emily."

"Annie?"

"Yes."

Emily turned to stare out the window. Softly she said, "I'll miss you."

Bullies

Linda Keller

You remind me of a fourth grader
who has a crush
on a little girl
you pull her hair
throw sticks at her in the playground
push her into mud puddles

She doesn't fight back
she twirls her hair around her finger
coats her fear in sugary syrup

I've been like the girl
in the playground
sweetly
collecting
the verbal bullets
you shoot at me
they're piled like hills around me

I've climbed on top of them
I see your inconsistency flags
your double message crowns
and your long bully robes

You can keep waving your pretend power swords
but you can't scare me anymore

you're just a shadow of the real monster
and I've already torn off his legs and arms

I'm rolling your bullets down the street now
so you can trip on them

Calculatin

♥

Carol Barrett

He got his nerve, walkin roun with his head up like he tryin to see pass the fog hangin over the Arkansas, his mouth shut tight as a grasshopper jaws on a blade a wheat. He jes be actin cool like I ain't got no right to know his business, shit. I ain't got no right to do somethin bout the rips inside me raw as pig liver, ain't got no right to ask him, Lord, ask him what goin on? Can't say why, what for, how long I gotta let him in the door like this, all stuck up like a cactus somewhere in Texas jes fulla hisself, walkin through my words like they some feathers come off his chest in this breeze blowin between us, his coffee steamin like the tar bumps they been patchin up on the streets for bout a year now they ain't never gon get done and he keep pourin more in, more steam and I was pleadin with that man to make him see what he done an Lord there was one time he was tryin to be so righteous and God-a-mighty I woulda kill that man if I'da been standin by the broom closet where I keep Mama iron, somethin bigger than his hand hangin so casual like on his belt, but it was hard to see, all them tears comin out my eyes, belly hurtin somethin terrible, froze up in a scream so long inside. Don't know if I coulda seen good-a-nough to kill a cockroach, I was tremblin and mad like a dog shut up a week and no water. I tell you girl, I seen somethin funny rise up in him, jes once, I could feel it twitchen that colla I press Saturday and I say to myself maybe he at leas gon say he gon stop it, even if he can't say he sorry to his woman so I try to quit my shakin and my hand come out and then he got right up in my face and he say KISS MY ASS BITCH.

Well, the air stop and everythin went limp as collard greens and I lean back on my heels to give the callouses some breathin room and then honey I jes walk through that space like there wasn't nothin between us, no name, no chile, no ford pickup, nothin, and I fill up the bucket, swung out the mop and scrub that floor like I was raisin Lazarus and I ain't once ask him what he done that for and I spit that soap over my bare feet backa my knees and my behind and that the last time I argue with that fool. He ain't gettin no mo, neither. Cause I been countin the things I need fa this life and that man don't figure.

A Friend's Confession

Gina Bergamino

She tells me
he fills up her body
but leaves her mind empty
& someday soon,
silent, the rage
will burst hard
and like a dangerous woman
she'll shout seven dirty words
and pull away.

Releasing

💔

Judith Serin

She knew she would have to break up with him and it broke her heart. He was so innocent, so unconscious when he hurt her. Like a child, a beautiful boy who was sure the world loved him. His big brown eyes ringed with luxuriant lashes would stare straight into hers, the hair that exactly matched the eyes falling in a thick fringe across his round, high forehead. He'd smile and plead confidently, as he had the night before, sure of being forgiven. "But Cynthia, I was just a little late, I lost track of time." And she had smiled back, the long distressing drive in rush hour, the exhaustion, the worry about her empty house, the hassle and sacrifice of leaving work early to make the movie, his movie that he wanted her to see. They beat behind her eyes, pulsing against the part of her brain that forgave him in his innocence, his childlike incompetence, his sweetness. She forgave him always. She was too tired to get angry. It was futile; he didn't mean to be unkind, why ruin what pleasure she could still get from the evening. And she loved him.

Perhaps it was Sophie's call that Saturday morning that did it. Sophie was his mother, hip casual, far too sharp and sophisticated for her unworldly, kindly son.

"Cynthia, you're there. Listen, dear, I've got it, just get pregnant. No really, I mean it, it will solve all our problems. He's so passive. You get pregnant and we'll make a big fuss, and you can move into a bigger place in the city and he can, oh, go to law school or something." Cynthia imagined her waving an elegant ringed hand in the air as she searched for a career for her chronically underemployed son. "I'll pay of course."

"Sophie, ah, thank you, but I don't think that's what he wants."

"Oh, what he wants. He doesn't know what he wants. He's so slow. Listen, darling, you've got to push him a little."

After Cynthia hung up, she burst into tears, surprising herself.

"Cyndy, Cyndy, don't cry. What's the matter?"

"Your mother wants me to get pregnant."

"I know," he replied, not a bit startled. Why hadn't he told her? "She thinks it would make me grow up."

Again that pulse in her brain. Why do you stay with him, he's hopeless, it will never work. And she cried because he was sweet and soft and sexy. Because, though she drove miles every week, since he was afraid of freeways, to see him in his tiny messy apartment instead of her comfortable, loved house she had worked so hard to buy; though he worked half-time as an usher in a movie house (inconvenient times that made it hard to get together with him) so that he, instead of Mama, could pay for his rent and food and spend the other half of his time doing absolutely nothing, as far as she could tell, unless she were there to nag him into some activity; though she was tired, dead tired of the exhaustion of this relation-ship and could see no future in it; though her friends thought she dated him for his looks only and were beginning to doubt her sanity; she loved him. Loved him for that very unworldliness so different from her job as a manager, loved him for his childlike delight in the world and confusion as to what to do in it, loved him for his sweetness, his always hugging and touching her, and for his immense joy in her, a warmer, far more exciting Mama who came to bed with him, surprised and appreciated him, and made him feel like a man.

"Cynthia, please don't. Why are you crying?"

"I'm afraid we may have to stop seeing each other."

"Why?" A thin high wounded cry. The terrified surprise and pain in his voice amazed her. It moved her with the revelation of his caring, but also confirmed her resolve. How could he be so sur-prised when she had told him over and over how hard it was for her to come here, how she needed him to visit her sometimes or for them to live together? He didn't hear, that's how he survived in his strange, limited world, he didn't absorb the information that would disturb him. And how could he expect her not to be hurt that he never heard her? But he didn't expect it, obviously. For him intentions were all, and toward her he always seemed to have the best of intentions.

His hand stiffened in hers. He wasn't breathing; she knew that his chest tightened into a rock when he was afraid. Poor dear. She stroked his hand, deeply regretting that she had frightened him with the truth. It made her so sad. The other pulse began in her body, the one that stuck in her chest, wanting to say the words, "I love you." She couldn't say them because he wouldn't say them back, only kiss her hand over and over and look scared, his breath tightening, so the words weighed down the air between them. She preferred that weight in her chest, rather than out in the world where it could harm everything. But still his sorrow needed some abating, and she was too much a Mama and too much in love not to, dishonestly, do it. "It's just so hard," she said. And then because he wouldn't hear or wouldn't understand the former. "I guess your mother depressed me."

He squeezed her hand. "You mustn't talk to her if she makes you upset. I should have said you weren't here."

"No, I like her." Which was true. She kissed his cheek, that dear sweet blooming boy, her age but so much younger, and knew how much he pleased her and that she must go.

Later he had a plan. It was unusual for him, all this action. Perhaps he had been spurred into it by the fear her words had sparked and they had buried under kisses and everyday activities. His plan was, like most of his projects, irrelevant to the world, but he entered into it with uncustomary energy. They would release balloons into the wind on the hill above his apartment. He must have gotten the idea by noticing the helium machine in the drug- store where they stopped to get her some aspirin. The balloons would have cards attached so that whoever found them would send the cards back and they would know where they had blown. It sounded like fun, she agreed, trying to lighten the heaviness of her thoughts. Indeed, depression sat on her like a cat, a large Persian who plunks herself down on your chest when you lie in bed, oblivious of your discomfort.

Later that afternoon they returned to the drugstore. She chose a white balloon, milky, with a purple squiggle of a design. He chose yellow which he insisted would be easier to spot. It was fun to watch the helium slowly pumping into her balloon. Its white turned translucent, then clear, the purple stretching in the middle to mauve. His was not so attractive filled, the yellow turning faint and blotchy, the wan color of illness.

"We have to launch them as soon as possible," he com- manded, "before they lose any air."

But back at the apartment she didn't know what to write on the card. He filled his busily, with lies, it turned out, about a junior high school weather project. "They'll be more sympathetic if they think we're kids," he explained. Finally she simply wrote, "Please return to," and his address.

"Why not your address?" he asked.

"Oh well, because this is where they come from." She didn't tell him it would make her too sad to receive the card one day when she was no longer seeing him.

He fussed with his card, carefully enclosing it in a plastic bag before tying it to the string. Why not put this sort of precise energy into planning a career, she wondered. "Hurry," he urged her. "It's getting dark."

She haphazardly wrapped string around her card and tied it on, ignoring his disapproval. That heaviness still sat on her and made her slow, uncaring. He hustled her up the hill behind his apartment. It was pretty up there at dusk, the houses glowing on the city's slopes, a few west-facing windows flaming orange with the last of the sun, and in the eastern sky a fading pink which stained the concrete skyscrapers downtown. "Here, right at the top." He tested the wind. "Face east. You count down."

She did, pausing to breathe between numbers, stretching it out, wishing it would go as slowly as the sky, still blue in the great bowl of its center, darkened. Ten...nine ...eight...seven (a slight awkward stumbling over the two syllables here) ...six...five...four...three... two...one (it was over, as inevitable as sunset)...zero." He released his string and the balloon shot into the sky, then, more slowly, it seemed, wafted east.

"Why didn't you release yours? You were supposed to release yours." His voice was peevish, genuinely angry.

"I didn't know. I thought you were going to countdown for me."

"They were supposed to go at the same time. You spoiled it."

"I'm sorry. Here. I'll do mine now." She opened her fingers which had been pinched on the string and felt no weight removed, only the release of tensed muscles. Off her balloon went, up, then east, following. They watched. His vanished first, but she thought she could see, with her better eyes, hers glint and circle in the sun for a long time after.

"Wasn't that romantic?" he asked, draping an arm around her shoulders. "But you should have let yours go with mine."

She continued watching, imagining perhaps, a tiny speck of circling light and dark near the horizon.

"Well, it's getting cold." He started down, noticing her absence halfway. "Hey, aren't you coming?"

"No," she answered, "I'm never coming down."

2%

❤️

G. Marault

So he says to me —
"But honey,
I'm so great to you
98% of the time.
Can't you overlook
that 2%
when I'm an asshole?
Doesn't it balance out?"
Well, let's see...

2% of the time
your one voice
is raised against me,
calling me
a cold bitch — a selfish cunt.

2% of the time
your one hand
is cutting off the blood supply
to my lower arm,
your 5 fingers
leaving 5 marks there
for weeks to come.

2% of the time
you're the one who could be called
a rapist,
if I didn't know you so well

and want you
some of the time.

2% of the time
you're one flaming,
drunken
lunatic,
your 2 hands at my throat,
and I'm so scared
I actually scream
before you set me free.

2% of the time
you're one faithless husband,
and I wonder
how many
diseases
you're bringing home to me.

2% of the time
you haven't a clue
how much I'd like to hurt you.

So to answer your question,
no.

Notes from the Ex

💔

Meredith Moore

he was a computer engineer.
i, a pet store clerk.
oliver, my husband, is the man i love.
and he is sleeping with his married secretary, patsy deirdre.

star trek

sometimes we still cuddle on the futon in front of the tv. i tell
myself, things are okay.
really they are.
"i love you," i tell my hero.
"sssh," he says.
with the remote control oliver turns up the volume of star trek.
it is the episode where spock must mate or die.

the deep abyss of night

ten o'clock. oliver not yet home from his late night meeting. i
wrap his dinner in tinfoil. i wash all the dishes, then dry them
before stacking them in the cupboard.
i vacuum.
i wear mascara.
i wonder if it is possible to enact a massive self-improvement
campaign before oliver returns.
every couple (i tell myself) has problems.
things are bound to improve.
a body grows weary of the workaday world; of a life without
pleasure; eons of loneliness. oliver walked into my pet store and my

heart and lent sparkle to a dull minimum wage life.

his mute embraces remain bittersweet.

i shall wait.

at 3:00 a.m. godzilla and gamara wrestle like lovers. i listen for cars in the dark. i ask myself, what kind of person drives around at this hour? answer: cheating scumsucking bastards.

i pack my bags; unpack them; pack them again. ultimately i am unable to write the farewell note, to walk out the door, for i am merely wriggling under the despotic thumb of dependency.

a little thing, adultery.

my eyes close.

the return of oliver

my eyes open when i hear his key slide in the lock. his dark shape floats into the bedroom and stoops to remove his shoes. sleepily i wonder, is this really oliver? or did he die on the road in some horrific car crash, and this merely his ectoplasm returning to haunt me?

"hello there, love object," i chirp. "how was the meeting?"

"okay. i'm tired," he pronounces, and rolls away, barricading me off with his shoulder.

astrophysics

the universe, according to scientists, is constantly expanding. everything that is, getting farther and farther apart. it is a relief to know there is a scientific explanation.

fiber optics

in the hollow leg of oliver's shoe tree, i find a hidden love letter from patsy deirdre. i read it while the tuna casserole is in the oven. i copy down her telephone number. i dial. it rings.

"hello?" i hear her despicable, breathy voice.

i call her again after the tuna casserole is out of the oven. i call her as frequently as possible over the next few weeks.

"why are you calling me?" she finally breaks down and sobs. "please stop calling me! what do you want from me? i have a small child!" she wails hysterically.

click.

there is a sour satisfaction in frightening her. i figure she deserves it.

the bitch.

the whore.

she'll probably give us all AIDS.

philosophy

le coeur a ses raisons que la raison ne connait point.

more fiber optics

late at night the telephone rings. by our sleeping ears it sounds like a siren. oliver explodes from bed. patsy deirdre calls to announce she is leaving her husband dwayne. he's drunk and roaring around the house, smashing the televisions. the baby is in hysterics.

patsy deirdre asks oliver to bring the jeep over to pick them up. after hanging up, oliver slips into his khakis and weejuns. i admire his grecian buttocks and hairy, masculine feet from afar.

i rise on my elbows. "can i help?"

"no," he shakes his head. "you sleep. you have to work tomorrow."

"please oliver," i say. "don't go. who knows what that dwayne person will do."

"precisely," oliver says, grabbing a sweatshirt, "why patsy deirdre needs me."

"you have a white knight complex," i tell him in disgust.

ethnocentrism

was it the aztecs who performed human sacrifice atop their pyramids, then ate the hearts of their still living victims?

soap operas

when oliver walks into the bedroom late the next afternoon, he eyes my bathrobe and the unmade bed. "didn't you go to work today?" he frowns, putting his hands on his hips. "didn't you get up at all?"

i shake my head. "guess i didn't feel like it. from now on," i say, "i'm living my life for *pleasure*, not pain."

oliver's eyes widen in horror and disbelief. "oh! there's no talking to you anymore!" he throws up his hands and leaves the bedroom.

equine science

consider the noble thoroughbred, asked to risk its life leaping over steeplechases, till its heart explodes and its big bones splinter with despair.

in the hall

near the umbrella stand and the coat rack, oliver tells me, "i've been seeing patsy deirdre."

sound waves oscillate through my body.

"tell me about her," i croak, my voice crawling from my larynx like a radioactive mutant.

"well," he sighs, "she's organized. she makes lists. her house is neat as a pin."

"then you are lovers," i deduce.

oliver nods. such events force me to think of things i would ordinarily be spared. i envisage patsy deirdre's rank, smelly, horrible crotch, full of flotsam and jetsam, next to thousands of migratory peni, not at all like my rosebud.

shopping

i buy groceries. i am moved by my own tragedy. i want to explain it to the checkout clerk, but must, perforce, bite my tongue.

criminal behavior

the next week the police knock on the door. they handcuff me and take me to jail. mugshots are taken. prints filed.

oliver bails me out at the station, but he refuses to speak to me on the way home. when we get inside the condo he suddenly bursts, "didn't you think they'd trace the calls?"

"i should have thought," i sob, sitting down at the kitchen table with a bowl of Fruit Loops.

oliver follows me.

"i've made a column of pluses and minuses," he announces, holding up a ream of computer paper as evidence. "the minuses outnumber the pluses."

"ANAL retentive computer geek!" i scream, hurling the bowl of Fruit Loops at him.

ivory milk droplets drip from oliver's handsome nose and sunburnt ears. he presses his fingers into his forehead as if under great strain. in a voice he probably believes to be as gentle as possible, he says, "i'm going to marry patsy dierdre."

i stare at the salt and pepper shakers.

"oh, oliver," i begin to cry. "you're such a jerk. and i wanted to have your baby."

he blinks at me without comprehension. i, too, find my non sequitur utterly fatuous. i put my head on the kitchen table and press my fists into my eyes. they beat like twin miniature hearts. this is me. this is me.

when i lift my head, he is gone.

the next day patsy deirdre phones to chat.

"you didn't even wash his dishes. you didn't appreciate oliver at all. well, he may not seem like much to you, but he makes me feel beautiful and loved!"

consider the roaming spotlight of oliver's pupil, casting a magic spell upon its lucky recipient, bestowing the gifts of love and beauty, then continuing upon its cortezian path of exploitation and plunder.

mistaken identity

mopingly i drag my feet from the pet store at night.

my only dinner companions, the ants in my kitchen.

but lo, behold oliver, miraculously rematerialized in the kitchen, drinking a glass of water.

i take off my coat and plunk down my purse. "so you're back. so you think i'll take you back so easily, huh?'

"i'm only here to pick up my clothes," he says. "and," he adds, "to give you thirty days' notice. i'm selling the condo. patsy deirdre and i are buying a house in the suburbs.

"now oliver," i wheedle. "why would you want to leave a swell gal like me?"

"but i don't love you anymore," he says, mystified by my unwillingness to accept this byte of data.

"i don't like reminding you," i tell oliver, "but you promised to love me forever."

oliver finishes drinking his glass of water and sets it by the sink. "i said i don't love you. did i mispronounce my words?"

i shake my head. this isn't happening. this is merely a case of mistaken identity.

this is not oliver.

this is captain kirk's evil twin.

farewell

"hey oliver," i say. "remember that book I read on nuclear war? it said there are enough nuclear warheads to destroy the earth hundreds of times over. those who won't die in the initial blast will starve to death in the nuclear winter."

"carrie," oliver murmurs, shaking his head. his eyes are hidden behind his gold-rimmed spectacles.

"imagine me crawling over the nuclear wasteland after the bomb, trying to locate your new address, chunks of the planet flying around our ears. i won't be able to tell you goodbye."

"tell me now," he says.

i look at my hands, concentrating on their lines and grooves.

"you'll be okay," oliver predicts cheerfully. "you'll find someone else. you're a sweet kid, carrie."

"yeah," i say.

consider salmon that batter their bodies leaping over waterfalls and rocks for that one final squirm in the gravel to achieve perfect union.

"have you found a place to stay?" he asks.

"i'll find one," i answer glumly.

"how do you feel?" oliver asks me, placing a fraternal hand on my shoulder. this is his last handout, last freebie, final payment.

"oh fine, fine," i answer briskly. "i've abdicated from the ranks of the unhappy."

he presses. "are you sure?"

"i'm happy!" i hear my voice rising. "i'm HAPPY! i shall die choking on my own laughter!"

one month later

oliver, my hate for you burns. i find myself standing in my kitchen, washing dishes with soapy elbows. all of a sudden, i mutter, ASSHOLE.

two months later

i hate the sound of the phone. it is the crack of doom.
it is dwayne, calling to ask me out.
"no thanks anyway," i tell him.
"please?" he begs. "don't you want to get back at them?"
i snap, "there are limits to my martyrdom."

zoology

consider camels, swaying across the sands, carrying within them enough to survive.

phil donahue

three years later i flip on the tv to a talk show. the subject of the day: impotence.
phil's glum-faced guests are patsy deirdre and spouse oliver.
oliver is lachrymose. he has put on weight.
patsy deirdre crosses her skinny ankles and proceeds to energetically publish oliver's shortcomings as a lover on the national airwaves.
this is great fun. i peel a banana and prop my feet on the coffee table and enjoy multiple belly laughs. i wipe a tear from my eye and think, poor, poor oliver.
the ultimate folly of not loving me.

denouement

now i am manager of the pet store, call home a warehouse loft, and am a human sexuality major at state university. i have been very happy.

i crochet afghans, breed angora rabbits and take belly dancing lessons.

of course, i blame myself, too, for what happened.

i wore him like a love amulet around my neck, which transformed overnight to a millstone.

what did i see in you, oliver?

your toenails, they were divine.

three years later the loss has become commodiousness. sometimes i put on my bagpipe records (you hated) and think there are many deaths.

i think of my cells, even now some are dying, others are being born. i read somewhere that every few years the epidermal cells are completely replaced. that means pretty soon, all the skin on my body you ever touched or kissed will no longer exist. you will exist for me only in memory.

perhaps, oliver, we shall meet again.

if not bumping shopping carts in the supermarket, perhaps in another lifetime. if shirley maclaine can get reincarnated, why not us?

perhaps in the sluggish frame of time and space, our borrowed atoms will reconvene and rise again as a bichon fise, a potted geranium, an igneous rock formation.

maybe time and space will neutralize our passions. my atoms then need not beet their tiny foreheads with infinitesimal fists in reproach, crying "fool! fool!" and experience deep pain and embarrassment in the association.

oliver, until then.

*h*ealing

Finally Breaking Training

💔

Alison Stone

A man who wastes your time
Steals pieces of your life.
— Zen proverb

My date lectures about the flute, toxic waste,
His colitis support group,
While I chew my macro meal
And think about self-nourishment.
I would rather be with the waitress
Or my sad, flamboyant friends who aren't good for me.
I would rather stand alone on Second Avenue
And let the stale breeze lift my hair.

I am tied to the chair
By years of training, the childhood chorus
of "be nice." I picture my nice, unhappy mother
And I hate both of us.
The deepest part of me is sick and I am sick
Of cruelty in all its forms
And my mute compliance.

I force myself to say, "I want to go now."
I leave him, still talking, and walk,
Gaining speed. I stop to give some money to a bagman.
He is shaking, and I want very much to be nice,
But I have laundry piled up and so
I save the quarters for myself.
They glimmer in my palm like luck.

A Circle of Voices

💔

Elizabeth Weber

I listen to a woman tell how the hollow vortex opened
in her chest and she begged
her lover to get off the phone and he
slammed her against a wall and told her

it was not his fault she was clumsy.
I listen to myself. I listen to a woman
tell how fear grows in her like death until
it pulls her into a blackness where voices race

all night. I listen to myself.
I listen to a woman sob how death
pulls her, there is no goodness in her
and how she took forty valium, felt

her head enlarge like a balloon.
And she listened to her sister
move in the next room and could not
rise and say, "Help me, I'm dying."

And she pinched herself all night long to stay awake
and woke in the morning to find the world and herself
still alive. I listen to myself
beat the air with my words and

I'm trying to give an equivalency
to the sound breath makes at 2 o'clock

in the afternoon in an empty house
where a man who I love has me by the throat and hisses

Shut up, shut up, just you shut up
and he loves me and why
am I so frightened?
What I listen for I can't hear:

When the breath stops, the voice
stops, and the woman who was me
rises, a witch out of the marsh,
out of the moon-struck sea,

out of my own self,
to take back what was lost:
breath and voice, something
that would let me sing or rest

the way the trees do after
the great winds come and take
leaves and branches, and whatever
else it can tear from them.

Words...Just Words?

♥

Rochelle Natt

I was in the bathroom putting on make-up when my husband burst in screaming, "Who told you that you could hire a baby-sitter?"

I had looked forward to my cousin's wedding for months—a posh affair, my first evening out since my second child was born. The black strapless gown that I'd bought was a real incentive to get my figure back. I was determined to leave the house looking glamorous, or at least stain-free, but my toddler-daughter kept yanking at me and my infant son yowled with hunger. After I fed him, he yowled with gas. There was no one to pitch in and help. My husband was napping in the living room and his parents, the only babysitters he would allow, wouldn't arrive until we were about to leave. I had phoned the teenager across the street and asked her to come help so that I could get ready.

"It's only for an hour," I said in a quavering voice. There I was, defending my expenditure of two dollars without considering the fact that we had abundant money and the reason why, was that I'd worked eight years and given my husband everything that I'd earned. All I could see were his flashing eyes, flaring nostrils, his fist punching the palm of his other hand. He had never actually hit me, but I had grown up in a home where my father ruled by his fist —or whatever happened to be nearby. My father once threw a hi-fi at my mother; another time he flung an ashtray in my sister's face and hit me over the head with a soda bottle. These nightmares were reawakened whenever my husband began to menace me.

Finally the doorbell rang. It was his parents. Although my husband continued to scream at me for "throwing around *his* money," my in-laws pretended that everything was fine. Perhaps to them it was. After all, they were treated to the same scenes every weekend when they came to visit, filling the void left by our friends who no longer came around. (Later some friends admitted to me that they stopped spending time in our company because they couldn't bear witnessing the way my husband treated me.)

It was a long drive to the wedding. For the entire trip he berated me and, when we got there, refused to pay for parking since I'd already "wasted *his* money." Because we had to cruise around for a spot, we arrived late. My mascara puddled under my eyes, but I pulled myself together and behaved as if I were deliriously happy. I didn't know that I had a right to feel otherwise. After all, I wasn't beaten...it was only words...just words. Also in those days I had the firm belief that if I could shape up and do whatever my husband wanted, I would have the perfect family life, the life that I'd always dreamed of. I was so busy trying to please him that I never saw how withdrawn, isolated and depressed he was, or how unfit a guide he was for anyone, including himself.

I had begun to experience distressing physical symptoms — my tongue hurt, my extremities often felt numb, I was cold all the time. The doctors, unable to find an organic cause for these symptoms, prescribed antidepressants. Now in addition to the symptoms, I had to cope with the side effects of medication — grogginess and loss of memory. I could hardly function and I slept most of the day.

My husband, who had become furious at the inconvenience to his life since he had to assume some child care and household responsibilities, called me a parasite. By then I had accepted his assessment and honestly came to believe that even my children would be better off without me. Soon after, I became suicidal and had to be hospitalized. After a few weeks of high doses of drugs, occupational therapy (sewing stuffed animals with a blunt plastic needle and making mosaic ashtrays), I was sent home to the same environment.

The psychiatrists couldn't possibly assess my situation since the information I could give them was not helpful. In childhood I had learned that truth was dangerous. The times I had shouted at my father, "Why are you beating me? I didn't do anything bad," he had pounded even harder. In order to survive, I pretended, even to myself, that I had deserved the beatings. They were *my* shame and I had to cover them up. Instead of telling everyone that my father beat me, I boasted about his physical strength. In the same manner, to my friends I glossed over my husband's behavior until it seemed acceptable, even meritorious. Also, my husband was able to function in his business. In non-intimate relationships, he seemed calm and friendly while I appeared increasingly nervous. I chattered incessantly, my hands trembled. How could I have known that he, too, was sick?

I remember being so physically and emotionally ill that I couldn't eat. Too weak to sit up, I lay on my psychiatrist's couch, telling him how ashamed I was that I couldn't balance the checkbook and how disgusted my husband was with me because of it. He didn't tell me that my physical state was the result of high doses of medication he had prescribed. Instead, he lit his pipe and asked, "Twenty years ago, when your brother was born, how did you feel about his penis?"

When I heard this, I knew he was useless to me in coping with the crisis in my marriage and that I had to find a way to help myself.

In a last-ditch effort, I combed the psychology section in the library and found the book, *Mental Health Through Will Training* by Dr. Abraham Lowe. Someone had kindly tucked in a list of free self-help groups. That night I went to my first meeting. The person who led it had numerous nervous breakdowns in the past. Through dedication to the Recovery, Inc. method, she had become well enough to go for leadership training, raise her two children, remarry, work her way through college and eventually to become a mental health professional. Both she and the other members of my group were great inspirations to me. At last I had hope.

The Recovery, Inc., method was easy to learn, but often difficult for me to put into practice. First of all, I had to learn to identify my own feelings. After a lifetime of focusing on others so that I could placate them, I wasn't aware of what my own feelings were. The next step was to learn a series of slogans which would help me avoid working myself up into a nervous dither referred to by the group as "temper."

For example, when my husband used to bang his fist on the dinner table when a meal wasn't to his fancy, I learned to ask myself, "What am I feeling?" The answer — "fearful temper." Then the appropriate slogans came to mind such as: "We do not need the approval of outer environment (other people)" or "stop the crying habit," and "do not respond unless you can do so with culture and dignity."

Lacking the emotional response that I used to supply, my husband now had no one to fight with. His rage began to boil over on others and at times was out of control. On one such occasion, he shoved a woman in a restaurant for refusing to put out her cigarette. He was so shaken by this experience that he also began to attend Recovery Inc. to learn to control his temper.

As we both became calmer, we each saw that we had been victims of dysfunctional members of our first families. His mother had suffered from severe depression, but instead of taking responsibility for her painful emotions, she had blamed them on her first-born son, my husband. He began to recall scenes from his early childhood — his mother screaming at him, "You're making me sick," then running to her room, sobbing, slamming the door; the long wait for his father to come home and side with her. My husband had developed deep rage against women, while long before, my father had groomed me for the role of the victim. If I hadn't found Recovery, Inc., both of us would still be locked into our old patterns.

We seemed headed for a marvelous future together except for one thing. Although my nervous symptoms were gone, my physical ones increased. Now that I was calm, the medical doctors took my complaints seriously. After all I had been through, I learned that I had two collagen disorders which were potentially disabling and had probably been tripped off by severe stress. I became furious and wanted revenge against my husband. Daily he was subjected to a tirade that echoed the trauma of his past. "You made me sick," I screamed. I became a harridan and found that I was as unhappy in that role as I'd been as a victim. The inner peace that I had learned to achieve through Recovery, Inc. was much more enticing. I once again threw myself into the Recovery, Inc. discipline, this time with renewed vigor.

I hear people say, "If you don't have your health, you don't have anything." The truth is, if you don't have your *mental* health, you don't have anything. Although I have serious physical problems, I am able to enjoy life far more than when I had a healthy body. I have the great pleasure of knowing that the changes in my husband and myself have allowed our children to become strong and independent, unlikely to ever fill the role of either abuser or scapegoat. Also, now there is a wonderful lightness between my husband and me. For example when I meditate, I play a tape called the Eternal Om. It's a solid hour of "Oooooohmmm, Ooooooooooohmmm..." I asked my husband, "Does this tape bother you?" He answered, "Noooooo."

Unfortunately, because of an increasing disability caused by my condition, I am writing this essay using a light pen that I point at a special keyboard designed for the handicapped. With each point, a red light flicks, there is a "ping" and another letter appears on the screen. It is a lengthy and painful process — a metaphor for my inner growth. However I now have the loving support of my husband, children and friends, and my own words which, through remarkable persistence, make their way out into the universe.

The Lone Woman

💔

Anne Meisenzahl

If she had a son
she would stroke his hair to wake him
now and tell him firmly that
he must never disrespect a woman.
If she had a daughter
she would write her a letter
telling her she must never disrespect herself
and tuck it beneath her pillow.
If she lived in the country she would
drag a sleeping bag behind her onto the lawn
and tell the stars she loves them.
She untangles the sheets
and resolves to sleep.
She dreams of stones and shattered glass
and delayed subways. In the morning
she works again. She calls her friend whose words
are like melted honey at the bottom of a cup
of strong tea.

Letting Go

♥

Tama J. Kieves

Lake Peekskill wrapped around the leafy hills of Westchester County in a hazel figure-eight. In June the surface of the mountain lake had been light olive and glittering; by late fall the water would turn graveyard to the brittle flame leaves that flew to rest there. Slowly the crunchy vestiges of summer would soften and saturate and find their way to the mud below. The lake would darken by winter, dense with the death that gave it life.

To the summer residents who came fresh from Long Island's chlorinated pools, the water was clammy and dark, and the musk of death and life was not pleasing. But to Liv it was wonderful, tickling with chill at first, then warm as a favorite quilt. The aroma flooded her with childhood summers when she had thought the lake was made of melted leaves and when she herself had smelled of the lake, had swallowed it, had it spurt through her nose like a dragon. Sometimes it had seemed her only friend, and this summer the lake became again a friend, the very best, welcoming her with deep memories and fresh currents.

In the lake, wrapped in green and sun, Liv could be herself, forgetting for a while that she felt ungainly and ashamed in a bathing suit. She felt no eyes crawling on the ripples of her arms and legs, only the dance of sun and water. There her white, whale thighs would lift, light and graceful, loved by the lake as through they were trim or toned.

Liv relished the solitude of the lake as the day grew cooler and sunbathers packed up their gear. She came in at four and swam until five, far out into the midst of the water where she could see the deep green hills around her and the brown, potato-shaped beach shrinking smaller and smaller. The tinier the land became, the safer Liv felt, as though she had placed a force field between her and the twig-like figures on the sand. Safe from young girls in color bright bikinis and men's leers crawling after them like bugs. Safe from her own stinging judgments.

Months ago Leo had yelled at her the first time she proudly told him how far she had swum. He grew flustered then critical, saying it scared him to think of her going that deeply into the lake. Eventually, faced with what he couldn't face, he'd stopped calling her. Now she smiled to herself as she put one arm slowly over the other into the gentle liquid. Going into anything that deeply probably scared Leo. She smiled, too, because the harmony she knew here could never harm.

Before now, it was rare in her thirty-two years that Liv experienced a sense of joining. More often than not people endured her the way the kids slouched in her composition classes for fifty minutes and not one second more. At best, "allowances" were made. Leo seemed to understand when she sat like a pumpkin at a dinner party, rigidly hoping that no one would talk to her and secretly saddened that no one did. But that June, Liv discovered a novel ease, a place where she could relieve her guard and simply be. She belonged in this lake. And now it was up to almost an hour a day, stroking slowly, surely, and giving in when her arms grew tired.

That was the trick she learned, the giving in. The relaxing into the water, the release it provided when her chest tightened or will weakened. Relaxing removed any edge of struggle. She was not afraid to feel her body sink deeper into the lake, feel water on her chin, her cheeks, even her eyelids.

The swimming ritual she'd established upon moving up here had begun in surrender, and surrender would always be a part of it. In May, when she'd found out about Leo's slim secretary, it took weeks for the pain to move through her and sift into her every day, to sit on her morning grapefruit, shuffle in with her papers, find a way into her bath.

Finally she'd torn away from the city one morning on the wild wings of impulse, soaring from pain. She sped the sixty-five miles to Lake Peekskill then burst out of the car, changed frantically and in a tired, vibrant fury swam out into the lake of her childhood. She hadn't planned on coming back. She hadn't planned on anything. She had just wanted to swim deeper and deeper out until she grew as tired, weak and futile as she felt inside. She would accept the darkness then, relaxing as the black totality came to claim her.

Only it hadn't come. The lake would not actively seize her like the press and pull of an ocean. No sputtering struggle or dramatic submission. The lake just let her be. And so she swam and swam until she was further than she had ever been before, wanly limp, the tears she had sworn not to cry leaking into the cool, smooth water. The green hills swelled, peaceful and shaded. A leaf had floated by. Under this sun and sky there were no expectations, judgments, criticisms, evaluations, instructions, struggles, deals. Nothing. Just quiet, vapid beauty, embracing, accepting, allowing.

And so Liv, limp and fluid, had floated on her back. For a moment she felt the lake ripple through her body and her breath met the sky suspended above her. Then she did a slow side stroke back. In a cloud of skinlessness, sky and water, she rested, connected. The desperation had passed and Liv knew something true. She was done with expectations, finished with struggle. It was this feeling she would recall when she decided to live at the lake.

The daily swim became a ritual and death was always a part of it, the part that subdued her. She could choose to let go whenever she wanted. That was understood. She could sink and wash it all away. She did not have to do or be a thing when she entered the lake. She could swim or float or sink. That was why she chose each time to live.

Leo didn't understand her leaving. He thought she was being dramatic and that she would be better off in Brooklyn where they lived. It was humid, but they had air conditioning. He thought they should see more of each other instead of less. But he conceded. Whatever way she wanted to handle it would be fine. Clearly he had said that grudgingly, but he had no other option. He had been seeing his secretary and he had been caught.

Angela, a fidgeting brunette, had come to Liv in tears at the house one May morning and told her everything, everything and more, while Liv sat stone-faced and grew fatter. She hated her husband. She hated herself. She could feel the seams of her cotton pants grow tighter and tighter; the sweat poured from her underarms. Angela's voice whinnied on while Liv imagined her high, firm breasts in a silky plum-colored camisole. No, Leo and his lies were exposed this time. Leo had to be nice. He had smudged his polished valor.

Liv's feelings of hurt and hatred were old, leaden and familiar like her thighs. They did not begin with this agonized brunette who coaxed Leo's slimy kisses or the redheaded waitress before her.

Maybe they hadn't even begun with her own explosive father, Liv wasn't sure. All she knew was that the pit feelings would always return. She would always lug the defeated child within her, deformed, helpless, withdrawn. Not good enough. She had raged against the skin on her body, her watery blue eyes and limp russet hair, the self she had always been, the self she had never loved.

After Angela's impulsive confession, Liv and Leo had gone out to sort out their lives over dinner like prudent people. Over lasagna, she remembered him sitting nervous and puny in the diner. He wore a vibrant blue canvas shirt, new cologne and his black hair slicked back. As always, he relied on magnetism. When they spoke of Angela, Liv looked away and stared at the gold lattice work upon the mirrors that hung on blood red walls.

Leo kept trying to win her with his smile. He apologized again. He looked remorseful, shaken, deflated. His sureness was gone, the false security that women loved, an aura that glowed around him like Vaseline. Liv had once loved that illusion of security, too, the suggestion of ease and certainty, the promise of a Prince Charming. But now the Prince sagged. He had piles of backlogged work in his office, no secretary, and a sunken quiet in his home. He had a broken image and a broken wife. Leo hated jagged edges and it showed.

The affair hadn't been anything, he said again. Just a passing thing. Just passing. Magic words. Supposed to take it all away, the pain, the injury. Just passing — not the real thing, not like their marriage. Just passing, as though nothing had really happened, even when he had gone to work animated and early, shaving with exaltation. Because for Leo, affairs were just passing. For Leo what counted was the permanency of marriage, no matter how thin that commitment wore.

And in an old way Liv half bought it, a resigned and heavy way. She had sensed the transience of the affairs while she had taken her years with Leo. It was she who met his family, she who held him when he felt fragile, she he put faith in like a steel anchor. So she stayed because in the end she won the prize. Leo would never leave her.

At the diner she had looked at the mirror to avoid Leo's eyes. From the lattice work in several cracked pieces a bloated face with shining eyes stared back. It began to cry. She hated the desolate hole within her. She felt like a pauper, collecting her scraps. "Oh, Livvy, Livvy Lou," Leo responded, a response more appropriate to a five-year-old. He darted to her side and dabbed a red napkin under her eyes, stroking her hair then pulling her dramatically close. "I love you," he insisted.

It was degrading how good the hug felt, the arms around her, the protection, the darkness. She hated herself for allowing him to hold her and allowing the rush of emotions that followed. The hug was a lie, so good, so warm. It sheltered her from the breasts of the brunette, Leo's distance these past few months, the bloated face in the mirror. The hug made it all go away — all go away, almost.

Still, after her first frantic swim and the peace that followed, Liv had decided to leave Brooklyn and Leo for the summer. She had the time off from teaching and the perfect vacation place. Her parents had kept up a summer house in Lake Peekskill. Liv had spent childhood summers there and, later, had often visited the town of ramshackle magic and snug wooden houses.

When she announced her plans for June through August, Leo visibly unhinged. He paced around the bedroom like a hungry tiger. It struck him as strange, he repeated over and over, that Liv would want to be alone. Liv could see that it unsettled him in some way he could not think to express; distance could be defiance. He grew childish as Liv packed, but he called Liv the child while badgering her with reasons to stay. She should go on with life, not step outside of it. What she proposed wasn't reasonable or normal. He finished with his favorite argument: Liv could not take care of herself.

She had continued to cram the old yellow suitcase with treasured books and tee shirts. She understood that Leo would never comprehend her desire for solitude or her wish for death to him. In the quiet spaces, she sensed he'd always been filled with a hideous premonition of danger, an imminent "something could happen."

And this time something had. During the summer, Liv came to love her morning walks, evening reads, and that which she had staved off all her life — being alone. Now she understood. She had always been alone. The same part of her which had shed Leo and his sordid affairs, had walked off in childhood to gaze at honeysuckles and bumble bees and to live beyond sick, cruel words and everyone who inflicted pain. She'd walked away from herself as well. Until now.

Over the summer, something else had happened too. Gradually and steadily Liv was losing weight. The lake was releasing her, taking her beyond the body she felt bound by all of her life. As she melted into the water day after day, the loose white skin she had seen as a deformity and a prison melted. Throughout the weeks she saw her arms and legs tone, brown and strengthen.

Swimming became addicting. The weariness of movement she'd always despised before transformed in the lake. She felt invigorated now by the aching of her tired arms and the gasping of breath in her chest. This pain was honest, something she could feel and face and stop by stopping. Not like the other pain, the unending ache burrowed beneath a mulch of remembrances. In the lake Liv merged these hurts, threw the hollow of her being into the stroke of an arm or the thundering kick of a leg. She swam hard to forge through, maybe to forgive. She could fight the water or lean into it, let thoughts and definitions go — rage and recrimination.

By the end of July swimming had become a religion, the lake, a holy place, a place of wholeness. In the middle of August, Liv called Leo to tell him she would not teach in the fall. She'd stay in Lake Peekskill until the cold set in. Then she would figure out something else to do. It was sudden, but she was sure.

He arrived that next weekend in a fury. The "experiment" had gone too far. "Are you goddam crazy?" he screamed. He flushed with indignation, glaring at her with disgust, for him an automatic look. But then he looked again. He stopped, quiet. Liv sat stonelike at the kitchen table, a pile of worn books forming a puddle about her elbow. She was thinner, firmer, brown. Neither asking his permission, nor wavering, Liv saw a sliver of recognition rip through Leo's picture of reality.

Fear made him ugly, lack of control always did. His face contorted in fury. He rampaged through the refrigerator, tearing out the ice cream, the Kentucky Fried Chicken. "Are these your friends? These your pals, Liv? Who the hell do you know up here? Do you know anybody? Are you just going to hole up like a rabbit? Like a goddam rabbit?" Liv froze like a rabbit, clenched inside.

He went on, as she tried to let the words fall away like she did the water when it was cold and shocking to her skin. But Leo's words and tone invaded her before she could shed them. They knew their way in; they'd been there before. Some had never left. Liv twisted the marriage band on her left finger. It had become loose like her clothing. She twisted inside, but instinct kept her motionless.

"What the hell is wrong with you anyway? Why can't you be normal, Liv? Come back to the city. We'll talk." Leo's face slackened with the promise of the old love. Liv desperately wanted someone to take all the loneliness away, the lapses between solitude, the clamorous moments of doubt. "I'll take care of you, Liv," he whispered. He reached out to touch his wife, but she withdrew. He would only love the old Liv. He would only love her need. And he would violate her, *make* her need.

"I have to go now," she said suddenly, solidly. Her voice felt foreign, but she rose. In truth, she had no idea where to go. Feelings rocketed inside her and the room, the kitchen where she devoured novels and wrote in her journals had become cramped. Leo was ruining everything. Suddenly her haven felt paper thin and her life insubstantial. Leo's words sprung bramble bushes within her, prickly recrimination, stabs of old pain. The walks, the swims, the lake — they all *did* seem like the visions of a crazy person, out of touch with the world.

Liv scrambled out the kitchen door and started the old Buick. She didn't want to walk to town. She wanted to drive; she wanted speed, power. She wanted the distance between herself and that man in the kitchen to increase to the point where he could not reach her, that man who knew her deformity and had kept her helplessness alive by loving it, nurturing it, then turning it around to torment her.

As she drove into town, she realized she had nowhere to go. Pain pounded at her. She drove past the shops, onto Route Six to the Kentucky Fried Chicken. Habit. An old instinct. As she got out of the car, the vinyl clutched at her, sticky with sweat.

She hurried into the building where the air was icy cool and thick with chicken. Liv got in line behind a blonde girl of about sixteen who wore a pink tube top, cutoff shorts and a bright gold locket. Goddess of the normal, what Liv had always wanted to be: friends, boyfriends, good at volleyball, the list went on. She wiped a tear from her eye before reaching the counter.

Leo's sneer as he went through the refrigerator loomed before her, ugly, his words, his tones. Shame and rage fed inside her again, her old cronies. They hadn't died after all. Liv willed herself to keep from crying and ordered the three piece box, even though usually she ordered the two now.

"Sure," said the pimple-faced boy as he smiled and put her order in. "Say, you've lost some weight, haven't you?" he asked. "You look nice." Liv smiled at the boy in answer to his question and took her chicken quickly.

She sat down and stared at the box. She could smell the spiced batter but she didn't feel hungry. She had only wanted to end the ache. Eating had always made her feel warm and nurtured, filling the edges of emptiness inside her. She watched him serve another customer. He had not looked through her. Instead he'd looked right at her. Someone had invited her into the world.

Liv checked her watch. It was only two, but she wanted desperately to be in the lake and swim far out to the spot where she could see the hills. Without another thought, she left the box of chicken on the table unopened. She was certain, proud, as she got into the car again, scanning the backseat for her suit.

She felt as she did in dreams, just like the first time she had arrived in June. Right. She changed in the beach house and headed toward the water, passed a clump of mothers and children splashing by the shore.

Savoring the water's initial chill, Liv began the long, slow strokes that carried her out, far into the greenness. The sun beat down strong at this time of day. She swam powerfully now, stamina thundering in each stride. She was alive as she had never been before despite shadows of sadness. She swam long and gloriously hard. Finally she stopped to look at the hills and sky and feel her beating breath.

Then as she began again, something momentous happened. The gold band that had come loose for a few weeks now, slipped off her finger and sparkled in the water as it began sinking slowly down. It shimmied like a shiny fish. She didn't stop it. Liv gazed at her pure brown finger interrupted by the narrow white circle no longer shielded from the sun. A chilling thrill shot through her and she swam on, sidestroking silently like an eel. The unopened box of Kentucky Fried Chicken danced in her head, Leo alone up at the house, the smile of the pimpled boy, the breasts of the brunette secretary and then her gold band like a shy fish going down, down toward the mud and the murk at the bottom of the lake.

She thought about the bottom, where the wedding band lay by now, how the muck below mixed with the olive surface in the sun; all was one in the lake, decay and shimmering life. And at the bottom of herself, she crumbled like dead leaves while in her upper reaches she shimmered like a ripple catching sunlight. With each new breath she felt promises flutter within her. She let a lifetime of broken ones go. Leaning back, floating, gazing at the blue horizon and hills leafy with life, Liv felt light and excited — lighter than she had ever been.

Death and Life

💔

Paula Legendre

Eternal Springtime

Rodin's Lovers

Lines etched in bronze.
"I am beautiful"
the scars in the sculpture read.

You, the man, rigid, solid, muscles straining.
Me, the fetal woman lying upon your chest
My femininity exposed for penetration
by every voyeur walking past.

Love is not solid like bronze.
It crumbles like the aged plaster making up
the "Eternal Springtime" of lovers entwined.

How do you know that we could sculpt
our feelings into something solid?
All my grand passions end up as dust.

—June 1988

And this is how our relationship started—a series of poems written
by one for the other.

I had known Joseph for three years; he and I worked together.
Our courtship officially started on a business trip to Philadelphia
where we were both presenting papers. Two Long Island Iced Teas

and a river cruise in a rainstorm were the fatal ingredients for me. On the dance floor, I kissed him and sealed my fate for the next two years.

When we returned from the trip, I had no intention of continuing the romance. I was engaged to another; Joseph had been dating a co-worker. But the taste of the passion we had shared in Philly remained with me, especially when Joseph left reminders in the form of cassette tapes, poems, and Toulouse-Lautrec postcards on my desk at work.

I finally took the plunge. Six weeks later when I telephoned Joseph to tell him I was coming to his home, I had the strangest feeling that my entire life would change. That premonition haunted me in the months to come.

That Sunday in late June, Joseph and his three children and my son and I took our first bike ride together along the Platte River in Denver. As we rode through the deserted industrial acres and the desolate landscape of oil refineries, I told Joseph of my desire of sharing a spiritual journey with a lover; of "going one better" like the D.H. Lawrence character I had fallen for when I was twenty. I also wanted to have another baby before it was too late. Joseph shared with me his desire for an "Eternal Springtime" of romance and of having a family. Our descent into hell began.

First, we got rid of the excess baggage. We discarded our previous lovers, and our children went off to our ex-spouses for the summer. We then had five weeks together. Five weeks like no other weeks in my life.

For the first time in years, I had no responsibilities except to get to work on time. I lived all my literary fantasies. I was Julia Mottram, running away with Charles Ryder in *Brideshead Revisited.* I was Elvira Madigan eloping with her Swedish army officer. When we rode the "Desert Wind" to Los Angeles, I was Eva Marie Saint seducing Cary Grant on the train in *North by Northwest.*

Even without the literary facet, the life we were creating together was a romantic masterpiece. Joseph and I explored the Platte. We walked through the barrio in North Denver. We drank champagne in his claw foot bathtub on Friday nights. And, during a trip to California, we pledged our love for one another on the windswept sands of Huntington Beach.

Every moment I spent with him was intoxicating. Each second was exquisite. The feel of his skin, the sound of his voice, the taste of his mouth—these all had the same affect on me as the Long

Island Iced Teas I drank when I met him.

There were signs then. Joseph's bank statement showing five bounced checks a week. His pile of unpaid bills on his desk. Our constant shopping sprees at department stores on the weekends. His borrowing of money from me because he was broke. His evasiveness about how he got custody of his children. The rumors I heard at work about his previous relationships. The seemingly unnecessary vindictiveness toward him by his previous lovers. The "I HATE JOSEPH" fan club, which Joseph himself started.

But these signs made me want to try to save him. After all, he had never known the love of a good woman, a wonderful woman like me. And my good salary would help to bail him out of his financial troubles.

Dark

Two Month Anniversary

We have been married two months today.

Instead of spring with its budding
trees and runoff from mountain
meadows covered with snow

I think about death.

Of trenches dug deep in mud
a smouldering, obliterated
landscape over which shells

explode and upon which the
debris of war and blown-up
pieces of once-whole men lie

What casualties will result from our union?

—November 1988

The nightmare began soon after we were married.

Joseph's children returned home five days before school started. Because they lived in Denver and I in Boulder, Joseph and I made an overnight decision to rent a house and get married. And we did.

In the process of moving two households and trying to establish a home, I got to know Joseph's children better. By then he had told me some of their terrible story — taken away from their neglectful and alcoholic mother, he'd had them for the past year. The oldest boy was twelve, epileptic, and was less responsible than my seven-year-old son. His second boy, John, was ten and had severe emotional problems. His daughter, eight, appeared normal on the surface, but suffered from daily screaming fits.

And I was going to save them.

Of course, these children needed a mother. And I was going to be such a good mother, too. What I didn't realize was that my husband also wanted a mother—he wanted someone to take responsibility for those three messed-up kids.

So I set off doing the same things for my new family that I had always done with my son—swimming and skating and bicycle riding, the family Christmas party and college basketball games. But the harder I tried, the more I failed.

I first began to realize this after the first month of John's "honeymoon" phase. After that time, the ten-year-old started showing his real hand and, from then on, crises rained upon us like the plagues of Egypt.

The day I found out I was pregnant, John assaulted a younger boy on the way to school, causing his victim to get stitches in his head. I thought this was terrible and told Joseph so as we went to the school to talk to the principal. Joseph told me to be more understanding of John's "special needs."

Soon John was stealing toys and jewelry from other students at school and from everyone in the family. He played with the stolen items at the dinner table to get attention. My stomach knotted every time I saw two or three unfamiliar watches on John's wrist. When I saw my sapphire ring on John's hand, I disciplined him for stealing, but Joseph blamed me for being too rigid in my principles.

When John's recurring encopresis returned, he left his pads of fetid bowel movements around the house. I told Joseph that this was a health hazard for the other children, but Joseph denied John had a problem and looked at me with contempt in his eyes.

The chaos of family life was also taking its toll on my son. One morning, I watched as my son stood in a puddle of John's urine to use the bathroom. My son's toys, given to him by his paternal grandparents, were either destroyed or stolen by John. My son was the true victim — and I was the one who had placed him in this unhealthy environment. To appease my guilt, I tried harder to save Joseph and John.

As I grew bigger with the baby, the situation with John escalated. I wasn't sure what the boy would do next. I felt as if a time bomb was ticking away inside me, and that I only had a little bit of time to get the family pulled together.

When I verbalized my concerns to Joseph he dismissed them with, "You're just catastrophizing."

I tried again. "What can we do to make this better?"

"It will get better."

"How? I want more than reassurances. I need details."

"It just will," Joseph said.

So I stopped talking and started hitting; the frustration building up and bursting under the terrible pressure. This action served only to accelerate my descent into darkness because I was attacking the man I loved. I finally chose to take my anger out on myself—by hitting my head against the wall.

During one of these episodes, I asked Joseph for help. "I'm going over the edge."

He said, "You go where you want."

Feeling totally abandoned, I banged my head against the wall again and again. Helpless, Joseph dialed 911. As the sirens approached the house, I pulled myself together, sat at the bottom of the stairs and waited for the humiliation that was sure to follow. As the paramedic took my blood pressure, she asked what she could do. I sobbed, "Nothing," for there was nothing she could do. I knew I wanted out, I knew I wanted to escape, but she couldn't save me. Joseph didn't want to save me. No one could save me.

Dust

Suicide

You ask, "Why do you think of suicide?
We just got married.
You're going to have my baby."

I answer, "We just got married.
I'm going to have your baby."

There are times
In the middle of the night
After Sunday dinner
In the afternoon
When you leave me.
Your body is there,
Your heart is not.
Your voice sounds like voices from my past.
Voices that always disappeared.

When I cry for help like a drowning swimmer,
Your words throw out lead shoes.
I can't tread water with the weight.
A knife to my wrist is my only life raft.

I've been out in the middle of the lake before.
I've never disappeared beneath the black surface.
I'm drowning now.
I'm afraid of the voices in the water
More than I fear the lake of my blood beside me.

—January 1989

I poured out my story to the emergency psychiatrist at the hospital. I told him about John and Joseph's denial about John's problems. I told him that I feared for my safety, my son's safety and the safety of the unborn baby. I told him about the frustration I felt in trying to just "contain" the situation at home.

The psychiatrist leveled with me. He told me that I had some decisions to make about my future. He advised me to leave the house for a while, to take the time to think things through.

After a few days of separation, I missed Joseph. My addiction for him soon blocked out the nightmarish events of the past few months. I telephoned him and suggested that John be placed outside the home to give ourselves some time, and to get John the help he so desperately needed.

Joseph responded to this crisis. He immediately placed John in a psychiatric hospital. During the hospital intake interview, I learned more about the disjointed life those children had with their father and mother, and how little their father had done to remedy their environment. I also heard about Joseph's own abusive childhood, and I watched him go blank as the questions probed deeper.

Once John was in the hospital, family life still revolved around him. There were visiting hours on the weekends and required therapy sessions for the family with John's attending psychologist. And these were the worst.

Since my son and I were the only ones in the family who would open up at the sessions, the therapist concentrated the family's problems on us—and we'd only been with the family six months. Joseph provided no support at all. In fact, I felt that he was glad that I was there to take some of the burden off of him.

In further sessions, I observed the same blank stares, the same avoidance tactics and the same blaming techniques in both of Joseph's sons and in Joseph himself. With this family's reactions, I didn't see much hope of improvement in the near future.

The longer John was in the hospital, the more Joseph attacked me. He degraded my college degree. He made fun of my Christian beliefs. He started blaming the other children's problems on my son. The family had fractured—the four Whitneys versus the two Legendres.

I quit trying. Every effort I made on behalf of the Whitneys sapped my limited strength as all my energy was going into growing the baby. I was operating only out of duty and honor, and I soon discovered that duty and honor don't go far without encouragement or appreciation.

In my pain, I found a new role model to emulate. Since Julia Mottram no longer fit, I opted for Sylvia Plath — the gifted poet who committed suicide at 31. I felt I only had one option at that point: I had to remove myself from the situation. Ah, but how? Moving out would be dishonorable, I thought — it would smack of quitting, and God knew that I was not a quitter. Staying, however, was intolerable. So that left only one choice. By "checking out," I could both leave the situation and leave it with honor. And I could get the baby out of it too. And my son? I was too distraught to worry about him.

With this twisted thinking in the back of my mind, I searched for some glass one Saturday morning when I had had enough. Removing a small piece from a picture frame containing a photograph of my son and me in happier times, I sawed at my wrist. Fortunately, the scratches didn't go too deep. Several hours later, I realized what I had done. I was scared. I was out of control.

Light

Death and life (excerpt)

On Saturday I played with glass, the light
Reflecting the secret thoughts of a soul dark
With pain. I've never felt so all alone.
What is there to life?
So I looked at death.
Thank God, I stopped and joined the living crowd.

I grope through the dark into the light
Leaving the crowd of suicidal voices to be alone
To say goodbye to death and embrace life.

—February 1989

During this time, a pair of guardian angels were watching over me — a medical doctor at work monitoring my pregnancy and my psychologist. Sensing my increasing deterioration, they conspired between them to knock some sense into my head.

"Paula, the baby and your son are your first priorities."

"What about Joseph? What about John and the other Whitney children?" I cried.

"They have a father. He should be taking care of them just like you should be concentrating on taking care of your son and getting through this pregnancy. You and your health are your first priority," they both advised.

Along with the priority setting, they outlined my other options. "If you are going to stay with Joseph, you'll have to take some medication; otherwise, you should move out."

At their insistence, and to exhaust all other possibilities, I consulted with a psychiatrist to go on antidepressants.

"Forget it," she said. "Any kind of medication might damage the baby. From what you've been telling me, your husband needs to take responsibility for his children, and you need to get out. *Now!*"

So with the Greek chorus of doctors granting me permission and chanting "Get out! Get out!" I finally took the steps to leave.

God, I looked forward to moving! My own place with my own son. Peace and quiet and waiting for the baby. My belongings safe

184

from destruction by Joseph and his children. The chaotic crisis over.

As I made arrangements to move, some of my depression lifted. I started feeling my own power surge back. I bought plastic dishes for the kitchen and some throw rugs for the bathroom. I was making my own decisions again.

I moved out in my seventh month of pregnancy. With my twisted ankle and a huge stomach, my son and I moved, carrying boxes up the stairs to a small apartment that looked out onto the Flatirons west of Boulder. My husband couldn't help because he felt sick to his stomach.

It didn't take long for Joseph to vent all of his anger onto me. Now that I was no longer attending the family therapy sessions, he had to face them alone. He had to cope with the three kids by himself on the weekends; John was home on passes then. Most of the conversations I had with him before the baby was born were angry and blaming.

According to Joseph, I couldn't do anything right. I spent most of those two months in tears. But I also spent that time seeking help, reading books on addictive love relationships and taking charge of my life. And within two months after my daughter's birth, I had gathered the strength to file for divorce.

The divorce was long and bitter. Joseph, enraged that I left and took the baby with me, conspired to win custody of our daughter. It was then that I regretted my suicidal behavior during the course of the pregnancy because that was the rock upon which he was building his case. Joseph also continued his taunting comments and his angry actions in an attempt to break me and prove me an incompetent mother.

After working all day and taking care of my son and the new baby, I had little left to cope with Joseph's abuse. But I knew that it would only be a matter of months until I was free of him, so I gritted my teeth and resolved to last it out.

I concentrated on my writing. I sent out the poems I had written during my marriage to editors and many of them were accepted and published. I finished a correspondence course in poetry at the University of Colorado and received an A-.

I also concentrated on helping my son regain his sense of worth and self-esteem. We took ice-skating lessons together. He submitted his poetry to several contests and won. We joined a church which not only gave me emotional support, but provided him a group of positive male role models in their Cadet (Boy Scout) program. And he and I enjoyed the new baby, the wonderful red-haired little girl who didn't seem to suffer from her months in the womb of a depressed mother.

Today, I see Joseph three times a week when he comes to visit the baby. Although I still feel a strong physical attraction for him, I know the price is too high.

After 35 years of trying to find myself, I feel like I am finally getting there. I have never been stronger. I have never been happier. I am pursuing my own goals and listening to my own voice. And I no longer need to seek out fantasies because nothing could surpass the reality I experience when I write and the abundance of joy I feel with my children.

Pedestal

You put me on a pedestal
And circled round me scanned
My form and figure, my design
Upon your gilded stand.

Not liking what you saw you took
The chisel in your hand
And chipped first here, then there to make
Me look like no man's land.

You took layer after layer
But when you reached my core
You could not break me down, my love,
No, not one small dent more.

Angered, you pushed me off that stand
A sledgehammer you found
You flailed repeatedly at me,
The rubble strewed the ground.

Until this day I never knew
That I was not revered,
But smashed to minute bits because
My love was what you feared.

—September 1990

Daily Lessons

Ahn Behrens

I am learning to live without you,
which sounds ridiculous
having never had you from the start.
My mind racing down streets
marked: DO NOT ENTER
spinning round deadly curves.

I pull eggs from a single basket.
Make omelets & soufflés
from the ingredients
of six separate recipes,
dye the rest a myriad of shades
& hide them all
through the town.

I am learning to listen
to the sound of a single dancer
so long ignored, I thought
she had died in childhood.

I stare full faced in the mirror,
ignore the two-headed stem
of an orange carnation;
the matching jade candles;
& Simon sounds
of twin children
playing in the yard
beneath my window.

In my cupboard
none of the stoneware mugs match.
I hang a widowed earring
from a silver chain,
plant orchids in the glass mate
of a missing slipper
& by afternoon I am able
to push your image
so far back in my mind,
it rests gently among
the petals of dried flowers
drained mute by age.

I am learning to live without you,
to savor the soft tones
of lace-like wildflowers
tamed in yesterday's sun,
able to shake off
the disorder of night dreams —
my mind still racing round
sharp corners, falling
down steep hills with you.

What's Good About the End

💔

Naomi Feigelson Chase

Zack called me this morning and cancelled our affair. First he cancelled our date for tonight. That's nothing new. But there was something new in his voice.

"So who are you sleeping with?" I asked.

"I'm not sleeping with her yet. I think we should just be friends."

"You and me?" I asked. "Or you and her?" Then I told him, "Don't bother answering. I'm hanging up."

***

So how do you feel? I ask myself.

Angry. Empty. Relieved.

It's true that I'm relieved. I'm glad to have myself back. I was such an insistent giver, he was such a reluctant taker. It was such a typical affair.

"You know I can't make a commitment." That was Zack's line.

"Not even for Friday?" That was mine.

Then I'd pull back, make sure I was busy when he called. If he said, "Four o'clock," I'd say, "What about six?" I'd fool myself I was keeping my pride. I thought I'd come to terms with this.

If I'd been giving someone else advice, I would have said, don't come to terms. They're his.

Instead I told myself, half a loaf is better than none. The problem is that love is not a loaf of bread. When you eat the one half, there is always the Kirlian image of the other half. You are still hungry.

***

Cheer up, I tell myself. You can't lose something you never

had. But of course you can. You can lose hope. You can lose fantasy. I always hoped Zack would see how wonderful I really was.

Zack would have some terrible injury. He would fall one day when he was out running and become temporarily blind. Calling me at 6 a.m., he would tell me he had just managed to stumble to the phone. For a week his eyes would be bandaged while I'd take care of him. I'd bring him to my studio. I'd sketch him, we'd listen to my favorite operas, *Turandot* and *Madame Butterfly,* we'd talk about art. When he took off the bandages, he'd see me again, a new woman; he'd realize how much he loved me.

***

I didn't need Dr. Mutter, my therapist, to ask me why Zack's eyes were bandaged. I asked myself.

Was it my age, because at fifty, I was ten years older, afraid Zack would look too close? Was I saying I wanted him to fall in love with the essential me, the soul? Did I realize he might as well be blind, since like Narcissus, Zack could only see himself? Why did I think I should take care of him? What did I get from this fantasy? Stupid, I replied, you made up the fantasy. You bandaged the wrong eyes.

***

What I've lost is the fantasy that I am part of a pair, the way Ted and I were before he died. Mornings I wake up and look out my window at the trees, the sun, and then it sweeps over me. I'm alone again on a vast desert. There everyone else, everything else, the travelers, the palm trees, the birds, even the mirages are in pairs.

***

In the beginning, we were friends. We should have stayed that way, at opposite ends of my studio couch, me piling things between us the way I did on our first date. The Sunday *Times,* the MOMA catalogue.

From his end of the sofa, Zack told me I was gorgeous. "So voluptuous," he said. "You look so good in that color. I want to paint you in that dress."

He went home with the belt so he could mix the exact shade.

I thought of posing naked with the belt around my hips. "Do me with a sketch pad. I'll draw you while you paint me."

"That's too equal," he said. He forgot about painting me though he did a sketch. I thought it made me look so enticing, it must mean he loved me, no matter that he said he couldn't fall in love.

***

You're an artist. You'll use it, I tell myself. At first, this is not a comforting thought. Then I take out my sketch pad and do Zack in Picasso's African Cubist style, half front, half back, half white, half black. I call it *Ambivalent Zack*.

That takes care of him. Now I have to take care of me. I should do a self-portrait. But how should I paint myself?

***

At first Zack mentioned several women he was dating. None of them was serious. I was much more interesting, he said. And once he slept with them, they bored him. He told the truth, but I couldn't hear it. I pretended he was faithful to me, though he never was. He was faithful to himself.

***

He couldn't accept monogamy.

"You make it sound like a religion. It's not like accepting Christ." I tried logic.

"Yes, it is. That's exactly what it is, a religion. And I'm an atheist," he grinned, blue-eyed and boyish, leaning over to kiss me on the neck.

I should have turned my back. Instead, I played therapist. "As an Irish Catholic, you're all messed up. It's the old Madonna/whore complex. You can't love women you sleep with. You can't sleep with women you love."

"Who's talking love? And you're not messed up?"

"Not from religion."

"You're messed up with me."

His analysis was better than mine. I was messed up.

***

"Oh, Mom. I hate him, that bastard. He should drop dead," my daughter Rebecca says when I tell her Zack and I are through.

How can you feel absolutely dreadful about life with a daughter like that!

I do not feel dreadful, but I don't talk about it. Everyone has troubles and most people think theirs are worst. It's hard to get a load off your chest when no one wants to hear it drop.

Here's this hurt, I want to say. I can't get rid of it. Looking up at the sky, I can't see what kind of day it is. No birds in the trees. No sun in the sky, just big black clouds. The one marked PAIN is lodged between REJECTION and LOSS. They drop to my shoulders. Everywhere I go I'm trapped between then. At night they squeeze into my bed on either side of me. I shut my eyes and think this is the worst way to be alone.

***

"Don't come down to my loft," Zack insisted on the phone the day we first made love. "I'm trying to resist you." He was already in one relationship that wasn't working. He didn't want to get involved.

"Please repeat that," I asked him. "You're in a relationship that doesn't work. And you don't want to get into one that does?"

"You're so linear."

"You mean I try to think straight and you think in curves."

"My relationships with women never work."

How could I resist thinking ours would?

***

Zack's almost bald on top of his head and when I met him, what hair he had was gray. I could see from an old California driver's license that he wore it long in the sixties. Now it's short. Last Christmas he became a blonde.

"Are you trying to trick Santa Claus?" I asked, when I saw his new color. "Are you going to do your nails?"

"If you can dye your hair, why shouldn't I dye mine?"

I knew then that he had met another woman, and she was younger.

Sometimes his hair stood straight on end as though he gave off electricity while he paced around his large studio in his khaki shorts and T-shirt, talking non-stop about art. At first I thought, is this guy nuts?

His corner loft had windows on two sides and it was full of light but light seemed irrelevant to Zack. He often painted at night and his work was more about color. I hate him, but I still think his painting has power. It explodes with color.

"It's Dionysian," was how he described it. "Like me."

"You mean you like to fuck," I said.

I learned a lot about painting from him. And a lot about myself.

***

Zack's literary heroes were Wilde, Mishima and Genet, not because they were gay, but because they lived on the edge. Zack was drawn to edges. The first time I went down to his loft, he climbed 12 feet up his exercise rope and hung by his heels. "I bet none of your other boyfriends can do this," he shouted down to me.

"None of my other boyfriends are monkeys," I told him to keep my mind off how gorgeous he looked, even upside down, in his running shorts.

Later he climbed out his fifth floor window and walked along the outside ledge, daring me to watch.

I'm terrified of heights, so while he gamboled on the ledge, I sat in his huge bare studio, trying to concentrate on how neat it was, the black floor scrubbed down, the large paintings leaned against the walls, the rope and weight-lifting bench smack in the middle, surrounded by a jungle of plants.

Just when I thought he's gone for good, he made a grand reentry. "Art's about taking risks," Zack said, jumping to the floor.

"You're a major flake," I told him. I was relieved he was back. "You're a fruitcake. Walking ledges may be risky, but it isn't art."

"What about Phillipe what's-his-name, the French highwire artist who walked up the World Trade Center?"

"That's different. That's performance."

"Oh, you're so bourgeois. It's just a bigger performance, a bigger risk."

"So the bigger the risk, the greater the art?"

"Absolutely. Sure. Art is pushing yourself beyond ordinary boundaries."

I told him knowing him took me far enough.

***

I pushed more than usual in my work. I'd been avoiding faces, especially my face. Instead I painted Zack.

I did a series of Zack portraits, a tryptich of Triathalon Zack: Zack in black biking shorts, leaning aggressively over handlebars; Zack surfacing from mean-looking waves, a water monster in goggles and bathing cap; Zack sprinting, pumping his arms, his muscled legs closing in on the finish line. I was hooked on the hero. Zack was what I got.

When I realized I couldn't draw the hero's face, I should have ended the relationship. I took a leap of faith, believing he was different than I knew he was. The risk of love is falling out of it.

I've started to look in the mirror and do self-portraits. Yesterday I did a double *After and Before.* I made the hair with cotton balls soaked in paint gray for *After,* orange for *Before,* and glued them on the heads. I found some old earrings in my jewelry box and stapled them to the canvas. Then I laquered the lips with nail polish.

After that, I did a series, moving the eyes around, experimenting with perspective. I got lost in myself.

***

Today I woke up thinking of Liu, the slave girl in *Turandot*. She kills herself for Calaf, the hero, rather than betray him to Turandot, the princess Calaf loves. Turandot distrusts men, since a man betrayed her ancestress. She gives Calaf the three-riddle test. He solves them and wins her. The plot is even more complicated. Like life, operas always are.

Liu's arias are beautiful. No matter. No matter how beautiful they are, Liu won't get the hero if he wants the Princess, because she's just a slave girl.

If this were a 20th century feminist opera, the kind I'd write if I were writing opera, she'd get him if she wanted him, though she'd be called a slave woman, not a slave girl. In my version, Turandot would know she couldn't trust any hero who'd let another woman sacrifice herself for him for love. Once she made him King, he might expect the same from her.

In my version, Turandot, the Princess who hates men, and Liu, the slave woman who loves above her station, would blow off the fickle hero; Turandot would recognize Liu as her equal; they would rule together, woman and non-wife.

***

"I want to paint those fields," I said to Ted ten years ago as we drove past miles of star-like potato blooms on our way to our last Long Island Thanksgiving.

"Next year bring your paints," he said.

Next year he was dead.

***

"So, I'll see you next month." Aimed straight at my heart, that was Zack's favorite exit line after we'd spent a night together, even though he'd call the next day.

"You're so predictable, you're getting boring. Try another tack," I'd say, trying to pretend it didn't hurt.

"Hey baby, don't count on me. I'm bound to let you down."

"Don't call me baby."

"I won't call you baby if you'll just say goodbye."

It was a refrain in a ballad. I was the pale lady who would die of love. He was the wandering knight.

I wanted to count on him the way I counted on Ted. I wanted him to be there when I woke up in the morning and when I went to sleep at night.

"You shouldn't fall for me. I'm no good and you're an easy mark."

Like Liu, I was a willing victim, but I blamed him. "So it's my fault I'm an easy mark? The bully blames the victim?"

"If you know that," he said, "get out of the way. Blow me off."

I wish I had.

***

I read a book about a woman whose husband leaves her after twenty-five years. She puts a good face on it. She goes to the museum. She does social work. She drinks a bottle of wine every night. I ask myself how is this like me.

***

I'm drinking too much. I haven't done that since Ted died.

Several months ago, I got raging drunk at Zack's studio and made a scene. I can't remember it, but Zack told me what I said, that I loved and hated him, that I couldn't stand the way he treated me.

True. I'd been saying all that sober. It registered more when I said it drunk. Zack was much nicer to me for a while, but it couldn't last. If you have to get raging drunk to elicit three weeks of affectionate consideration, you know this augurs ill for a relationship.

***

Last night I dreamed of my garden, I'm walking through purple tangles of waist-high nasturtium, crawling among the tomato plants, breathing their rank smell, touching the fuzz of enormous squash leaves, their vines overrunning the paths.

I'm standing in a field of white potato blooms. The starlike flowers trail over the dunes to the sea. I follow them to the water's edge.

I miss lying in bed with Zack, wrapping my legs around his body, the feel of his skin pushing past the horizon and floating back. I miss the way he stroked my arm, touched my breast.

There may be a scientific explanation, or maybe a psychological one, but I've never heard anything that makes it clear why you want to touch one person and not another. With animals, it's smell. "Le peaux," is what the French call it.

***

I knew there was someone else months ago, after Zack dyed

his hair. He got so much nicer and after that, so much less, I couldn't explain it if I wanted to. There are some things no explaining can make clear.   ***

"Hey, I miss you. Let's have dinner. Let's be friends."

This is Zack's message on my machine tonight, a month after we broke up. I'm furious. There's no phone in my studio, so when I came home at night, I'd look expectantly for that flashing green light. I was just getting used to it not being Zack when he called today and left that message.

His tape answers when I call him back. He's got new music. Last month it was something funky by The Five Blind Boys. Now it's Vivaldi, "Fall" from "The Seasons." A rare tape with the original instruments.

"Screw you," I want to tell his machine, "I gave you that tape. Give it back. Along with *The Love Poems of William Butler Yeats* and *The Architecture of the Italian Renaissance*. Give back the button that says 'Nixon Cares' and the pink and blue Lucite watch that looks like a Volkswagen. Give back the yellow plastic solar fan you clip on your lapel and the holy medal of St. Sebastian pierced by 100 arrows which you did a painting of. Give back the humidifier I hoped would make you think of me blowing in your ear at night."

I am working myself up into a fine rage. I would like to take those gifts, pile them in the middle of his studio, jump on them, douse them with kerosene and set them on fire.

I try to think of something clever and nasty to say about dinner, about friendship. Vivaldi's "Fall" is over, and so is Zack's tape. I hang up.

***

I'm going to rewrite all the opera plots from a feminist, third-world perspective and illustrate them. I'll do faces, too. All the heroines will look like me.

After Turandot, I'll tackle Madame Butterfly. Here's a white male mistreating a third-world woman, pretending to marry her, deserting her, returning with his new American wife to take away Butterfly's child. Poor Butterfly. She kills herself.

Poor Mrs. Sharpless. If she were smart, she'd realize this guy will find her stale in no time. He'll ditch her for an oriental mistress.

In my version, Mrs. Sharpless sees it coming. She and Butterfly join forces. They accuse the Lieutenant of perjury, bigamy, wife-abuse and kidnapping. He is court-martialed, gets four concurrent terms of 100 years. Mrs. Sharpless and Butterfly add a couple of rooms to Butterfly's pad so each can have her own wing. They take joint custody of the child.

Broken eggs make omelets. Love is the greatest risk to take. Broken hearts make art. I'm calling my book *NEW ILLUSTRATED OPERAS FROM OLD PARTS.*

***

Eventually, Dr. Mutter says, you have to deal with the memories. When I woke up today, it was snowing. I think of the two women in white with white umbrellas that Zack painted last year during a snowstorm and the painting he gave me, another snow painting, a woman in a green raincoat with a big red-brown umbrella. I thought it looked like the Japanese print on my wall, the tiny doll-like figure with the parasol and the snow coming down on the curled trees. When Rebecca saw it, she thought it looked like me.

I remembered the walk from the subway to Zack's studio last winter after the blizzard. Coming to meet me, he appeared in the distance against a streaked gray sky, his blue wool cap pulled down over his ears, his hands stuck in his jacket pockets. It's painful to remember how happy I was.

To get out of the wind, we trekked through the wasteland where last summer we saw Annie Mae, the circus elephant. I crawled up the hill on all fours with Zack pushing me. In my fur coat, I felt like an animal grabbing at roots. I wanted to stop right there and make love on the snow, in the dry leaves, in the middle of a lost world.

***

On certain winter days, the light is like early summer evenings just before sunset. In summer at dusk, Ted and I sat outside, under the pine trees, drinking wine, listening to bird cries.

***

Think of trees, the way they possess the earth, the way they were here before us and will be here after. Rebecca says there's a certain something in chlorophyll that resembles a compound in the blood. So it's not just poetic fancy to think we're the same stuff as trees.

I remember the sycamores at Pyramide in France when Ted and I were there on our honeymoon, the pale green bark like skin and dark patches, the same trees inside the Museum of Modern Art when I went there with Zack.

***

I go to my studio and spread drawing paper over the floor. Then I sit down on it and outline the lower half of my body. I lie down and as best I can, reaching and squirming, I outline the rest of me. From my collection of studio junk, from odds and ends, whatever I can find, I start filling in my paper self.

I glue old beads and discarded jewelry on my arms and legs, adding layers of paint, and, as that dries, odd cloth and paper scraps. An old bird's nest I found last year becomes my heart. I add a bit of cracked eggshell. I spend the day building myself up with paper and paint, leaves and feathers.

I paint my face with silver paint so it's half face, half moon. Finally I sprinkle gold and silver sequins on my crotch. I'm finished. I title my variegated self *APHRODITE FROM OLD PATCHES*.

***

I am going to New York for the weekend to see my children. Last night, lying in bed after I'd packed, I heard a loud crack and thought a tree limb had broken off. It was ice crashing to the ground.

This morning, it was still dark when I left the house to the rush of water down the gutters. There were so many large puddles on the sidewalks, I had to walk in the street.

From the train window, I see a pond that's half frozen. Or is it half thawed? One bird is walking along on the ice. Another is already swimming.

Why I Stayed
(An Essay About Leaving)

💔

Kay Marie Porterfield

"I'm in the driver's seat, and I'll be the one to decide when and where we stop," my husband of ten years said as we sped through the mountains that last Fourth of July weekend I spent married to him. Car windows rolled up, he continued to drive through one small town after another for two hours after I'd told him I needed to use the restroom. The evergreen trees, blue-tipped with new growth; columbines and black-eyed-susans — all merged into a blur as we snaked our way down the road, picking up speed. Before long the reality outside lost immediacy as my focus centered only on the stabbing pain in my bladder and on how I was going to make it home without wetting myself. Jaw set, he drove on.

After two more requests I gave up. How simple it would have been for him on this so-called pleasure trip to pull over. I shifted in my seat and crossed my legs.

"Selfish bitch," he muttered. "You can't do anything right, can you? I don't need you. There are plenty of other women..."

As he continued the tirade which had after years become a litany, I focused on my own thoughts. Why was he always compelled to work so strenuously at making life insufferable for me and for himself in the process? There was no way of knowing. Why had I stayed sealed in an emotionally abusive relationship for so long? Maybe that was a question I could answer.

Four years after the divorce, I'm still uncovering answers. Along the way, I've had help. Some women friends tell me it was mostly *his* fault; the rest of the blame belongs squarely on the doorstep of 4,000 years of patriarchal history. Others refuse to believe my past. *Those* women who stay and take it aren't college educated professionals like us. My marriage must have been an aberration, temporary insanity, which has nothing to do with who I am now. The rest scold, saying that there was no excuse for staying. Perhaps not, but during that time there were many *reasons* which, given the distorted context of nightmare logic, seemed perfectly valid then.

Seeking them has been a process as time-consuming and painful as I imagine stripping away my own skin layer upon layer might be, this exploratory surgery of my psyche. I cautiously biopsy past the obvious, scraping down to the place where the deeper, if less flattering, causes for remaining lie, slicing down to where hidden they wait, curable but lethal if undetected.

Theoretically, I could have walked away from the relationship at any time. After all, I was completely self-supporting and our finances were separate. Genetic entanglement wasn't a factor; we shared no children. Except for occasional objects carefully aimed to miss me and thrown across the room for theatrical effect, physical violence hadn't surfaced in years. He wasn't twisting my arm, only my heart. Yet like too many women who are victims of psychological abuse, I chose to make the best of a bad situation, to convince myself it was normal.

Why *did* I endure a decade of rage? In the first place, he wasn't overtly abusive when I met him. Witty, charming and a marvellous lover when he wanted to be, he made me happy at a time when I had few clues about how to nurture myself. Only occasionally did the tyrant inside him surface during our courtship and, even then, his anger was rarely aimed at me. When he grew furious at the I.R.S., his ex-wife, his boss and the dean of the graduate school he attended, I rationalized that he was a strong-willed man of conviction, that his anger was justified. It was a turn-on, setting off a high-pitched longing inside of me.

On our wedding day I pledged "for better or for worse," and I meant it with all my heart. When worse came to worst and hoof and horn appeared, abiding love became my potion against the rage-filled incantations he spewed at me and his repeated threats to see other women. This transforming elixir wasn't found in the pages of *Modern Romance* or even *Cosmopolitan,* but was instead a recipe from *1 Corinthians* and *Beauty and the Beast*. I concentrated on the good days, which outnumbered the bad, and waited for the miracle of reconciliation to work.

Growing up, I had learned that love covered the worst of sins, containing and concealing them like a one-size-fits-all garment. I expanded to love him despite his flaws, then to love him *because* of those flaws, since they gave me an opportunity to practice the virtues of humility and forgiveness. Slowly I turned from lover into holy whore, unaware that stretching to accommodate the hard, hot bulk of a wounded man's fury isn't emotional growth or a way to sainthood.

I prayed for patience, choosing to remain frozen in our dark ritual alchemy of dominance and submission in order to redeem my half of the human race. The nights spent cringing on the bed while he raved at me, I did penance for sins committed by women past and present — Medusa, his mother, ex-wife, old lovers and any witches missed by the Spanish Inquisition. "We're not *all* like that," my contrite and constant presence said. "I am a *good* woman." Yet because I didn't fully believe it, I continued to accept the humiliation he inflicted as my due.

If my husband was to be my tour guide for inferno, I resolved to be if not a happy camper, a dutiful one. In Girl Scout days I'd memorized all there was to know about loyalty. (Emotional abuse wasn't covered in the handbook.) Long after my trust in love wore thin, I persisted, determined to trade that placebo for a merit badge in tenacity. To leave would be admitting defeat worse than stopping piano lessons for lack of talent, or not pursuing a Ph.D. even though I was once accepted into a doctoral program. Besides, I convinced myself, I couldn't very well walk away after we'd been through so much together, the concentric circles of fire and ice that made the matrix of our marital Hades.

I stuck it out over the years, certain I would be a better person for it, certain *he* would be a better person too. He needed me, he begged, to take away his pain from childhood sexual and physical abuse. And so I struggled to heal this man whose broken soul bled battery acid. Feeling sorry for him and ignoring my own wounds, I shifted shape to become a sin-eater, earth mother, high priestess. Sprinkling tears and chanting apologies, dancing evasions on the drum head of his anger, I performed one exorcism after another.

And he *was* getting better, I told myself, because at least he didn't hit me anymore. After a severe beating at the very beginning of the marriage and a few subsequent slaps and shoves, he didn't have to — I was terrified of his anger. Well after our wedding, I learned that he had battered his last wife throughout their time together, most brutally when she carried his child. Clearly that was proof, I felt, that he loved me more than he had loved her, that I was a better woman than she was. When he reminded me of how ferociously he fought back his urge to hit me, I thanked him for using only words as weapons, for leaving only invisible scars.

Later I stayed because he blamed me for his temper so often, eventually I believed he was a monster *I* had created. Perhaps, he and his outbursts were a figment of my imagination. Just how does one divorce an imaginary being? In the crucible of suffering and self-sacrifice, I found a small seed of omnipotence which I chewed on, eager for emotional sustenance. If he were a demon I had conjured from the depths of my own shadow, *I* was the one with the power, the evil witch. To undo this perverted magic never seemed as simple as simply leaving.

When the intoxicant of self-delusion wore thin, when my daemon lover glittered with wrath, hard-edged as obsidian, I feared him, yes, but I was *more* afraid to be without him. He held enough fierceness inside for two, and I was certain I needed his savage rage to defend me. So he became my champion, my mercenary. A damsel in distress, I stayed blind to the fact he provoked most of the dangers he claimed to protect against. His terrorist attacks aimed at me were the price of rescue.

For a time, I used him as antagonist, certain I required his viciousness as a goad to achievement. Without that paradoxical prod of insult and injury moving me to covert resistance, I was aimless. Since childhood I had learned to employ my father's taunts as a spur for sullen excellence. Now defiantly I achieved recognition in the world outside while at home I cowered and secretly raged inside, wanting to kill him at times. Ashamed of those murderous fantasies, I believed myself mad for having them, and therefore, even more needy of his protection — this time from myself. In desperation I tried to be a better wife.

When I did consider ending the marriage, I rationalized that I was one of the lucky ones, better off than most. To reveal the parody of marriage I played out would draw attention away from the women's issues that mattered, away from the women who *really* needed help. I knew a great deal about the depth of their suffering because I'd written articles on domestic violence for years. Rather than identifying with the pain of battered women, I felt superior to them.

The few times I attempted to reveal the character of my marriage in therapy, support wasn't forthcoming. In one instance he verbally abused the counselor, and we were asked to leave. Most of the time, though, the issue of emotional terrorism was ignored. After all, he was a social worker and I had a degree in counseling; our marriage *couldn't* be the living hell I claimed it to be. My story defied all logic, not to mention raised real issues about the mental health profession as a whole.

Finally my frame of reference blurred until his insults and threats became a condition I accommodated like the dull pain of an old war wound. I endured through the time he ordered me to the doctor to beg for lithium for a bout of manic depression he had conveniently diagnosed, claiming that drugged, I would be easier to live with. I held my ground when the doctor assured me I didn't need a prescription but a divorce. I stood pat when the man who claimed to love me called me crazy because I still grieved a week after my mother's death. Turning a deaf ear to the epithets, I paid his back taxes, expanded my repertoire of oral sex techniques. I had made my bed, and I would lie in it.

In the end, to leave meant facing the reasons why I had stayed all those years, reasons which promised to make me feel more ashamed than remaining in the relationship and in denial. To walk away meant admitting just how wrong I'd been to love him in the first place. Initially I hadn't understood the depth of his anger or the impact it would have on me, but I *had* shuddered with delicious dread and followed this man who enticed me with his sweet bad-boy attitude. I had *volunteered* to go along for the ride.

In the initial stages of the marriage, at least, I felt a subtle thrill from living with a man on the edge. Rather than masochism, which derives satisfaction from being victimized, mine was a frisson triggered by *potential* danger, and by the subsequent relief of escaping unscathed each time it failed to completely materialize. It was the seductive lure of horror movies at the drive-in and beyond. Balancing on the precipice without falling off became my test of immortality, the intoxicating excitement of a near miss, easily mistaken for love.

At least my life wasn't boring, I told myself. There were the adrenaline rushes and the constant throbbing ache of an ulcerated heart to let me know I was alive. *I feel pain, therefore I am. If I leave him, will I cease to exist?* Finally there was the flood of relief which mimicked peace of mind — until the next time.

Physical violence is an obvious, black/white, either/or issue — chronic emotional battering is not. It slowly eats away at reason and self-esteem from the inside, spawning an insidious collusion between victim and victimizer. No human being — female or male — is completely immune from this spirit-deadening dance. Perhaps that is why so few people are willing to openly acknowledge the extent of domestic psychological terrorism in our culture or the damage it causes.

Self-blame is self-defeating. I didn't consciously set out to fall in love with an emotional abuser and I didn't ask for or deserve the humiliation I received. Neither did I determine the societal mind-set which dictates women, good women, must keep their mates happy at all costs, often at the price of their own human dignity.

At the same time, taking responsibility for my own choices has been a critical part of my healing process. To concede that I chose to act on the initial attraction and afterward made daily decisions to remain in an emotionally abusive relationship is a difficult thing to do. It has been a necessary thing to do. Only when I stopped trying to understand my husband's motives and focused on self-understanding, could I break free from the enthrallment. Only then could I know that the high-pitched longing I still occasionally feel in the presence of a sweet bad-boy isn't a mating call but a warning.

> *"There are plenty of other women..."* On the mountain road four years ago, somewhere between that nameless place and home, I knew what he said was true. There were other women who would tolerate his outrage. There will always be other women. If they wanted him, they could have him, I decided. That day's indignity wasn't the worst I'd endured, but I resolved it would be the final one. After that the rest came easily. Four words were all that were required to break the spell, four words to forge my own declaration of independence: I DON'T LOVE YOU. And it was over — except for the soul searching.

Renaissance Summer

Magi Stone

Skidding into delayed adolesence
My man, high in his heat, looks elsewhere
For greener ferns to sear.
Unbraided ends of myself hang limp.
What is left for me, but days so long
That hours push against the length of them.
I reconsider old values, passing years.

The convergence
Of the Medieval perspective point is a lie!
There is no true horizon.
It is easy to get lost.
The chosen road of my life narrows,
Crumbles at the edges, S*T*O*P*S.
Sun and clouds
Seem to divide the sky into equal pieces.
An unfinished woman
I must reconstruct myself;
Search for a new fate.

I have the woman of the bones
Cast yarrow sticks
Amber shafts of my fortune darken the ground.
Armed with hours of prayer
She chants to wind spirits low and gray.
My new life is established on
Quilt-comfort melodies of Mother Goose songs;
Reminding me no one owns grief or pain forever.

Clay remembers the hands that made it.
Beauty locked deep in bones emerges remolded.
I ensilk my legs in green stockings like stems;
My hair the color of apricots.
Now I am ripe enough to begin.

About the Authors

Renee A. Ashley won a 1990 Kenyon Review Award for Literary Excellence. She has received two Fellowships in Poetry from the New Jersey State Council on the Arts, as well as many other prizes. Currently she teaches creative writing in New Jersey and New York City. Her poetry collection, *Salt,* earned her the 1991 Brittingham Prize for Poetry and was published by the University of Wisconsin Press.

Mary Shen Barnidge, a Chicago poet and performance artist, avoids wearing name tags, party hats, seat belts and corsages. Her most recent book is *Piano Player at the Dionysia.* She writes poetry because she cannot play the piano.

Carol Barrett is a faculty member of The Graduate School of The Union Institute in Cincinnati. Her poetry has appeared in over fifty literary magazines including *Woman Poet, Fireweed, Conditions, Bloodroot* and *Daughters of Sarah.*

Ahn Behrens, a freelance writer who lives in the wilds of New Jersey on the edge of Manhattan, also works for Signet Books/The New American Library. Her poetry has been published in a variety of places including *McCall's, Earth's Daughters* and *The Buffalo News.*

Ellen E. Behrens, who received her MFA from Bowling Green State University's Creative Writing Program, has been published in *Fiction, Paragraph, Antithesis* and other periodicals. An assistant editor for *Mid-American Review,* she is currently completing a novel set in her hometown of Clyde, Ohio.

Gina Bergamino lives in Germany where she writes full-time. She is working on a collection of poetry under a grant from the

Ludwig Vogelstein Foundation. Her work has appeared in many literary magazines including *Black Bear Review, Poetry Motel* and the *Wisconsin Review.*

Norma Blair is a Michigan native, mother and grandmother. She has been published in *Beyond Science Fiction & Fantasy, Ouroboros, Thin Ice* and *Wisconsin Review.*

Karen Bowden lives in Phoenix, Arizona.

Ann Bronson is forty-six years old and is the mother of two children, ages seven and nineteen. Working around them, she has been a writer for twenty years, although she claims sometimes she didn't know it — often for years at a time.

Marilyn Elain Carmen, who has written as Aisha Eshe, is widely published in the U.S. and in Canada in journals such as *Heresies, Black American Literature Forum* and *Sing Heavenly Muse.* She is a recipient of a 1990 Pennsylvania State Council of the Arts Grant based on her book, *Blood at the Root.* Currently she is working on *A Walk Out of Water,* an autobiography. She lives with two cats and her teenage daughter in an apartment shared with the sun.

Marie Cartier has published in *Pudding, New Kent Quarterly, Focus, Edios, Heresies, Sinister Wisdom, Kalliope* and the anthology, *More Golden Apples.* She is a 1984 recipient of the first Creative Writing Fellowship in Colorado. Currently she attends UCLA, in their MFA Screenwriting Program.

Naomi Feigelson Chase is the author of the books, *Listening for Water* and *A Child Is Being Beaten: Child Abuse in America.* Her fiction has been published in *Lear's, Plainswoman* and *A Wider Giving.* She has received several awards for her work.

Elayne Clift writes articles, essays, poetry, and travel features which have appeared in over two dozen publications. A regular contributor to *New Directions for Women* and *New Jersey Woman,* she has won awards in the 1990 Writer's Digest Competition. She lives in Maryland with her husband and two children.

Donna Decker is a poet and writing teacher who is originally from New York and now lives in Wisconsin by way of Florida, where she recently earned her PhD in English. She is working to heal abuse on many different levels, and is interested in writing choreopoems as well as performing her poetry with other media.

Denise Duhamel has been published in *Ploughshares,* the *Ontario Review,* the *Massachusetts Review* and *Southern Poetry Review.* She is a 1989 recipient of a New York Foundation for the Arts fellowship. Her chapbook, *Heaven and Heck,* was published by Foundation Press.

Eileen Elliott was born in 1960 and grew up in Toms River, New Jersey. She received a bachelor's degree in journalism and anthropology from Syracuse University, and is now enrolled in the graduate fiction writing program at Sarah Lawrence College.

Barbara Foster, an assistant professor at CUNY has been published widely in poetry journals and anthologies in the U.S., Canada, Australia and Great Britain. She is the author of *Fobidden Journey: the Life of Alexandra David-Neel* (Harper & Row, 1987).

Nancy Lott Gauld is the mother of five. She has worked as a secretary, a bookkeeper and a junior high school English teacher. Although she has been writing "forever," only recently has she been submitting it for publication.

Elizabeth George is the author of the epigram in Laurel Speer's poem.

Phillis Gershator lives in the Virgin Islands. Her poetry and reviews have appeared in various anthologies and magazines including *The Patterson Literary Review* and *Caribbean Writer.* She is the author of a chapbook, *Bang Bang Lulu.*

Suzanne Grieco is a twenty-seven-year-old freelance writer. At the University of Pittsburgh, she garnered a BA in Fiction and an acute distrust of large, athletic types. She has lived in Queens, Long Island, London, Philadelphia and West Palm Beach, not necessarily in that order. Her work has surfaced in *Seventeen, Byline, The*

American Poetry Association Anthology and various small magazines. She is resolved to never again be suckered in by a *GQ* jawline.

Susan Hawthorne is the editor of three collections of fiction and poetry: *Different Writings by Women, Moments of Desire* and *The Exploding Frangipani.* She is co-author of *Silver-Tongued Sapphistry.* In 1989 she was awarded the Pandora Florence Janes Award for Outstanding Contribution to Women's Publishing. She lives in Melbourne, Australia.

Barbara Ittner, founder and active member of the Denver Women Writers' Support Group, has facilitated classes and workshops in expressive writing and journaling. Recently she served as a contributing editor of the anthology *Rhymes, Rituals & Reasons,* published by the Voices of Women Press.

Nancy Izawa is a Canadian-born resident of Molokai, Hawaii. Two marriages and four children have contributed to her autodidactic/ feminist education. She is a poet and photographer with four self-published books.

Linda Keller was born in Hackensack, New Jersey, in 1953. She graduated summa cum laude from Fairleigh Dickinson University with a BA in Social Work in 1975. She currently lives with her husband and son in Denver and is the author of two collections of poetry, *You Can Stop Longing* and *Here I Am.* She teaches writing and drawing to express feelings at a variety of schools and corporations.

Tama J. Kieves is an award-winning short story writer and poet. Currently, she writes profiles of courageous women and is at work on *This Time I Dance,* a non-fiction book exploring her personal breakthroughs in leaving behind common sense (and a law degree from Harvard) to go steady with the muse.

Willa Koretz studied poetry at Harvard's Young Poets Program in 1971. A dancer and ritualist, she can be seen nationally in readings and performances incorporating poetry, ceremony and the language of dance. She lives in Oregon, delighting in the wet, green earth.

Paula Legendre graduated with a BS in Mechanical Engineering from the University of Colorado. She has been a technical writer for eleven years. Her literary work has been published in *Meditations for the Divorced, Just Between Us, Cokefish* and *Feelings*.

Lynn Leone is the author of *Tangents,* a chapbook. Her poetry has been published for the past fifteen years in journals such as *Prairie Fire, Red Flower, Impetus* and *Different Drummer.* Her favorite things are beaches, money and attractive, intelligent gentlemen.

Karen Leslie is the pseudonym of a licensed social worker and alcoholism counselor who closed her private practice four years ago in order to write and teach writing and children's literature on the college level. Her features on dreams, incest, sex addiction, sports and family life have been published in the *Ladies Home Journal, First for Women, Mothering* and *Men's Health.* She also authored a chapter for *Dreamtime & Dreamwork* published by Tarcher.

Iris Litt has been published in a number of literary magazines including *Bitterroot, Stone Country, Lacuta* and *Poetry Now.* She lives in Greenwich Village where she makes a living "writing-to-order."

Ceil Malek has been a writer and editor for ten years. She currently teaches writing at the university level and is the single parent of a nine-year-old daughter and a seven-year-old son.

Chris Mandell is from Boston. She's a preschool teacher, violinist, portrait artist and poet.

Genevieve Marault lives in Maplewood, Minnesota.

Cris Mazza's books of short fiction include *Animal Acts* and *Is it Sexual Harassment Yet?* Her first novel, *How to Leave a Country,* will be released in 1992 from Coffee House Press. Mazza's fiction has been published in over thirty journals and anthologies. She is the Writer-in-Residence at Allegheny College in Meadville, Pennsylvania, and also resides in San Diego, California.

Yona Zeldis McDonough was born in Chadera, Israel and grew up in Brooklyn, New York. Educated at Vassar College and Columbia University, she lives in New York City with her husband, Paul A. McDonough, and is at work on a novel about the life of Mary Magdaline.

Anne Meisenzahl has lived in New York City for the past six years, where she has worked as an adult education teacher and curriculum writer for alternative schools in the South Bronx and Manhattan. She is also a visual artist.

Beverly G. Merrick teaches at the Institute of Public Law at the University of New Mexico in Albuquerque. Her work has been published extensively and she is the recipient of several poetry awards.

Meredith Moore, a teacher and a full-time mother, writes fiction as much as she can. A Berkeley graduate, she is a cat lover and a pretty good vegetarian cook. Her work has appeared in *Elephant Ear* and *Nerve Nob*. She's also a veteran of the war between the sexes and is the proud owner of every self-help book ever discussed on Donahue.

Caitlin Morrell recently graduated from the University of Wisconsin-Eau Claire with a BA in English/liberal arts. Presently she is spending her time job-hunting and writing.

Rusane Morrison teaches English and English as a second language at Berkeley High School and is a member of California Poets in the Schools. Her work has appeared in various small press publications.

Rochelle Natt could brag about her widely published poems, short stories and essays in literary magazines such as *Negative Capability, The MacGuffin* and *Story Review*. She could boast about literary awards and the inclusion of her work in several anthologies. However, she prefers to thank her children, Charles and Heather, for their often-sunsolicited criticism which keeps her striving and humble.

Jo Jane Pitt has been writing ever since she could write and remembers "pretend" writing before she knew how to shape letters. In recent years she has published in the *Greensboro Review, Cosmopolitan* and *Coraddi.* In order to support her writing habit, children and cat, Mayberry, she teaches freshman composition along with some freelance work.

Kay Marie Porterfield is a college-level writing instructor, drummaker, rabble-rouser and writer. She is the author of *Violent Voices: Twelve Steps to Freedom from Verbal and Emotional Abuse* and *Keeping Promises: The Challenge of a Sober Parent.* In addition, she has written two books for teenagers: *Coping with an Alcoholic Parent* and *Coping With Codependency.*

Vickie C. Posey has a BFA in visual art from the University of Tennessee at Knoxville and in 1988, completed an MA in English Literature from North Carolina State University. Currently she works for a creative literacy program called MOTHERREAD, writes articles for *Suzuki Family and Teacher* and is co-editor of the newsletter for the North Carolina Group of the Jane Austen Society of America.

Pamela Pratt has been published repeatedly in *Sinister Wisdom, The Minetta Review* and *The New York Native.* Her work is also included in *Lesbian Love Stories, Vol. II* (The Crossing Press). She is the director of In Our Own Write, a reading series at the Lesbian and Gay Community Center of New York.

Elisavietta Ritchie lives in Washington D.C. and by the Patuxent River in Maryland. Her seven collections of poetry include the prizewinning volumes, *Tightening the Circle Over Eel Country, Raking the Snow* and *The Problem With Eden.* The latest anthology she has edited is *The Dolphin's Arc: Poems on Endangered Creatures of the Sea. Flying Time,* her first fiction collection, is due in 1991 from Signal Books. She has won two awards from The Poetry Society of America and four Individual Artist Grants from the D.C. Commission on the Arts.

Elspeth Cameron Ritchie, M.D., Elisavietta's daughter, is currently the division psychiatrist for the 2nd Infantry Division in

Korea. She has had poetry and prose published in *The Radcliffe Quarterly, The Journal of the American Medical Association, Military Medicine, Washington Woman* and other magazines.

Candice Rowe has published short stories, essays and poems in *Apalachee Quarterly, The Monthly* and *Pale Fire Review.* She's a part-time instructor of English composition at the University of Massachusetts/Boston.

CarolAnn Russell is an associate professor and poet-in-residence at Bemidji State University where she codirects the Headwaters Writers Conference. Her first book of poetry, *The Red Envelope,* was published in 1985. She is now working on two new collections.

Joanne Seltzer has published poems in a number of literary magazines and in three collections of her own: *Adirondack Lake Poems, Suburban Landscape* and *Inside Invisible Walls.* Born in Detroit, she has lived in upstate New York since 1960.

Judith Serin has been published in a number of poetry and fiction anthologies including *Love Stories by the New Women* and *Dear Gentlepersons: A Collection of Bay Area Women Poets.*

Nina Silver is a counselor, Reichian bodyworker and singer as well as an internationally published writer. Her poetry, non-fiction and fiction on feminism, sexuality, humor and the natural sciences, has appeared in numerous magazines and anthologies: *Gnosis, Green Egg, Jewish Currents, Wanting Women* and *Women's Glib.* "I'm not so *nice* anymore," she reports, "but when I was, I used to be in *lots* of *relationships* like this."

Barbara M. Simon is a poet and teacher of writing who lives and works in Baltimore, Maryland. She is the assistant editor for *Maryland Poetry Review.* Most recently her work has appeared in *Only Morning In Her Shoes.*

Mary Crescenzo Simons has been published in *Plainswoman, West Wind Review, California Quarterly, Paragraph, Cosmopolitan, Playboy, The Writer* and numerous other journals and periodicals. Her work is included in the anthology, *Women in Exile,* and has won awards for fiction and poetry.

Laurel Speer, who lives in Tucson, Arizona, is the author of four collections of poetry. Her latest is *Cold Egg.* Recently her poetry has been published in *Iowa Woman, Centennial Review, Denver Quarterly* and *New Letters.*

Alison Stone was one of three new poets chosen for the Women Poets at Barnard Reading Series in 1988. Her poems have appeared in *Poetry, The Paris Review, Ploughshares* and other magazines. She is currently editing an anthology of spiritual poetry.

Magi Stone is one of the founding editors of the *South Florida Poetry Review.* She gives "hands on" poetry workshops in both the private and public sectors. For the past few years she has been a staff member at the Suncoast Writer's Conference.

Sharon F. Suer was born in Philadelphia in 1952 and still resides there. She writes newsletters and educational material for a life sciences indexing and abstracting publisher. Her poetry has been published in a number of small press journals.

Patti Tana is a professor of English in the SUNY system and the author of two books of poetry: *How Odd This Ritual of Harmony* and *Ask the Dreamer Where Night Begins.*

Cheryl Townsend edits *Impetus,* a literary magazine from Stowe, Ohio. Her poetry has appeared in *Amelia, Feminist Voices, Pearl* and a number of other publications. She has four chapbooks available from various small presses.

Nancy J. Wallace received her BA from the University of New Hampshire. Her poetry has been published in *The Christian Science Monitor, Appalachia, Wisconsin Review, Memphis State Review, Atlantis: A Women's Studies Journal* and elsewhere.

Elizabeth Weber teaches writing at the University of Nebraska in Lincoln. Her book of poems, *Small Mercies,* was published by Owl Creek Press. Her poems have been published in numerous small magazines including *Swamp Root, Calyx* and *Puerto del Sol.*

s.l. wisenberg has been a reporter, au pair, amusement park portrait artist, standup comic, trainer of civil disobedients and an English teacher in Nicaragua. Her work has appeared in *The New Yorker, Wigwag, Kenyon Review, Calyx* and other magazines.

Fabian Worsham, who teaches creative writing at the University of Houston Downtown, is the author of two chapbooks: *The Green Kangaroo* and *Aunt Erma's Country Kitchen & Bordello.* Her work has appeared in a number of literary journals.

Marilyn Zuckerman has published two books of poetry: *Personal Effects* and *Monday Morning Movie.* In addition to appearing in literary magazines, her poems were recently included in *Ourselves, Growing Older* from the Boston Women's Health Collective. She is the recipient of a PEN Syndicated Fiction Award.